1987

PLATO'S PROTAGORAS

a Socratic commentary

B. A. F. Hubbard &
E. S. Karnofsky

With a Foreword by
M. F. Burnyeat

The University of Chicago Press

The University of Chicago Press, Chicago 60637
Gerald Duckworth & Co. Ltd., London NW1

Published 1982
University of Chicago Press edition 1984
Printed in the United States of America

93 92 91 90 89 88 87 86 85 84   5 4 3 2 1

Library of Congress Cataloging in Publication Data

Hubbard, B. A. F.
    Plato's Protagoras.

    Includes the author's English translation of Plato's
Protagoras.
    Bibliography: p.
    Includes indexes.
    1. Plato. Protagoras.   2. Protagoras.   3. Socrates.
4. Sophists (Greek philosophy)   5. Ethics.
I. Karnofsky, E. S. (Ellen S.)   II. Plato. Protagoras.
English. 1984.   III. Title.
B382.H82   1984   170   83-18122
ISBN 0-226-67034-1
ISBN 0-226-67036-8 (pbk.)

Typeset by Input Typesetting Limited, London
Printed in Great Britain
by Ebenezer Baylis & Son Limited
The Trinity Press, Worcester, and London

Contents

When two go in company, one sees before the other.

Homer, *Iliad* 10.224–5

Foreword

M. F. Burnyeat

This book is that rare thing, a real contribution to education. Tony Hubbard and Ellen Karnofsky have conceived an entirely new way of presenting a masterpiece of philosophy and literature. Their excellent translation of Plato's *Protagoras* is backed up by a commentary which has the special feature that it is written from beginning to end as a series of questions. The questions are so arranged as to lead the reader on from one problem to the next, not haphazardly but building at each stage on the answers given to previous questions. The reader is made to think, and to think for himself, and then to think what his previous thoughts imply for the next issue. This approach is not merely valuable in itself. There is good reason to believe that it is in perfect sympathy with the spirit of the original.

Of all Plato's dialogues the *Protagoras* is the most vigorous presentation of Socrates at work in philosophical discussion. The action of the dialogue is a confrontation between Socrates and some of the most famous intellectual figures of his day. He argues with them; he reduces them to perplexity by his knotty, abstract reasoning; he parodies their own very different methods; he exposes their pretensions to have important knowledge to teach – all this in his most pugnacious style and with the savage irony which Plato, no doubt rightly, always made a prominent feature of his portrait of Socrates. Socrates' chief adversary in the discussion is the eldest and most distinguished of the gathering of intellectuals, Protagoras, and the issue between them, to state it in its broadest terms, is the nature of virtue: what it is and how it is to be acquired.

Foreword

Anyone who thinks he knows the answer to these questions will find that Plato has anticipated his presence among his readers. He has made Protagoras the spokesman for a number of views typical of 'common sense' or 'ordinary morality' in fifth-century Athens, and it is not difficult to find twentieth-century equivalents for the beliefs which Protagoras defends and Socrates attacks. We still tend to think, for example, that a person may have the wisdom to know what to do in a difficult situation and yet lack the courage to carry it out. Wisdom is one virtue, one quality to admire in a person, courage is another, and we do not expect them necessarily to go together or to be possessed by everyone to the same degree. If we belong to this class of reader, the *Protagoras* unrolls as a drama which challenges us to radical reflection on our values and assumptions.

If, on the other hand, we are uncertain where we stand on such questions, perhaps uncertain even how to begin thinking about them, Plato is prepared for that also. He will take us, as Socrates takes the young Hippocrates for whose benefit the discussion is held, and invite us to arbitrate between opposing views and opposing arguments. He will make us appreciate the inevitability with which a simple seeming question ramifies into others and has to be reconsidered, time and again, as further, connected problems come into sight. Above all, in Socrates and Protagoras he gives us two deeply opposed styles of thinking and discoursing about fundamental issues. About all these things Plato expects his readers to make a considered choice, each on his own behalf.

But of course it is one thing to see that Plato wants his reader to be an active participant in the discussion, another to stir oneself to a genuinely active reading. It is so easy, and certainly pleasurable, just to read the dialogue through without really stopping to think. What the authors have so splendidly done with their 'commentary by questions' is to compel, encourage, and most importantly to help the reader to be an active participant at every stage of the proceedings.

The questions are both systematic and wide-ranging. Literary and philosophical considerations are shown to be intertwined, as one would expect with a dialogue which is

Foreword

at one and the same time a masterpiece of philosophy and a great work of literary and dramatic art. Readers who feel themselves inexperienced in literary and philosophical skills will find that they can do much more than they had realized. The questions, if tackled seriously, will show the way, awakening ideas and sensitivities which may previously have lain latent and unused. That awakening is of course the great educative purpose of the Socratic method of questioning portrayed in the dialogue and now extended by the authors to the commentary on it. But even the most seasoned scholar, who has read and reflected on the *Protagoras* many times, will find that the questions open up fresh and stimulating lines of inquiry. In sum, it does not matter whether we are old or young, experienced or inexperienced: this is a book that should be welcomed into schools, university classes, private studies – wherever genuine education is sought and valued.

Robinson College, Cambridge   M.F.B.

For our parents

Preface

It might be supposed that the authors of a book know what the book is about and for whom it is intended. But we have in fact found the purpose of this book no less difficult to define than Plato's own intention or intended audience. Looked at in one way, the *Protagoras* is a literary and dramatic masterpiece, and an entertaining satire on the sophistic movement. Alternatively it can be seen as a punishing attack on rhetoric as a means of education: for in this dialogue we see the great master Protagoras make an impressive and plausible speech, only to have his ignorance of those very excellences which he professes to teach exposed by Socrates' mercilessly exact cross-questioning. By contrast we are shown two faces of Socrates himself. The Socrates we find at the beginning is a man of conventional morality, who shows an almost avuncular concern for the moral well-being of the impetuous Hippocrates; but in argument we see a man who is so devious, willing to make such apparently outrageous claims, that we can understand why Aristophanes took him for a sophist. It is as though Plato wanted to show both how different from the sophists Socrates really was, and yet how similar to them he appeared. From yet another point of view this is a serious philosophical work in which are propounded the unity of virtue and the Socratic Paradox that virtue is knowledge so that no man does wrong willingly. Moreover the sheer variety of argumentation and subject-matter make it possible to think of this work as itself constituting a course of instruction, but of a different kind from the type of course which Protagoras has for sale.

Perhaps, therefore, one of the most important features of this commentary is that it brings these disparate literary, polemical, philosophical and didactic elements together and helps the reader to relate them to one another. Hence

Preface

although it resembles the traditional commentary to the extent that it consists of text together with a section-by-section analysis, it takes a much broader view of the text than most commentaries on Plato. Nor have we aimed at that Platonic ideal for commentators, an exhaustive and definitive interpretation. This commentary is designed not to persuade learned scholars, though we hope that it has some interest to them, but to enable the text to operate on the reader as Plato operated on his students. It is thus primarily a teaching document, cast almost entirely in the form of questions. Were the reader to write down his answers to each question, he would have a commentary, though not the only possible one. The reader, then, should produce his answers, in whatever form they take, ideally from discussion with others, or simply by thinking them through by himself. We hope that the student will learn from this book a good deal about the *Protagoras*, about Socratic method and Platonic thought, and about the intellectual life of Classical Greece. But more important, we hope that he will develop his skills at exegesis and criticism, whether the object of his studies be a philosophical treatise, a historical document or a work of fiction. This general purpose has dictated the exclusive use of questions, in preference to a discursive commentary with 'questions for discussion', as is usual in student editions. Only by reading the dialogue actively, by constantly responding to the problems raised by the text, will the student learn the basis of all serious reading, that no text, fiction or non-fiction, should be allowed to pass through the mind without hindrance.

There are three recent translations of the *Protagoras* available: W. K. C. Guthrie in the Penguin Classics series (1956), Martin Ostwald's revision of Jowett (Bobbs-Merrill, New York, 1956) and C. C. W. Taylor in the Clarendon Plato series (Oxford University Press, 1976) with extensive commentary. This translation cannot hope to improve on these in accuracy or in general intelligibility. If there is a criticism it is that these elegant novelistic renderings tend to obscure the true character of Plato's literary art, which is not that of a novelist but that of a dramatic raconteur with an astonishingly varied literary palette. We have therefore tried to emphasise this sense of a man brilliantly telling his story to a friend, and at the same time to reflect the many subtle variations of style which Plato uses. Nevertheless the main justification of this translation lies in the way in which we hope the book will be used. For this reason we have chosen, in the more closely argued passages, to confront the reader with the full difficulty of Plato's literal text, rather than offer a more placid idiomatic rendering.

The problem facting the translator of Greek – what to do with untranslatable words like *sōphrosunē* or *hēdus* – has been solved by including the transliterated Greek word in the text. We have given the English word in italic followed by the Greek word in parenthesis. This use of Greek in the English text introduces the reader to a Greek word or reminds him of it after an interval. This system, too, allows us to vary the translation of some Greek words in accordance with the context. Once a Greek word has been introduced, its English translation is occasionally italicised without the Greek, to encourage the reader to recall the Greek. Finally, we cite, or re-cite, the Greek word where it is being specifically considered in the commentary.

This raises a problem. Greek is an inflected language in which the ending of a word varies with its case, gender and number. To reproduce exactly what is in the Greek text would confuse the reader who does not know Greek. But to ignore these differences will rightly offend the Hellenist. As a compromise, we have retained the nominative case throughout, but observed variations of gender and number whenever reasonably possible. Thus *dikaios* is the Masculine form of the Greek adjective which means *just* (a just *man*). Just *men* (the masculine *plural* form) is *dikaioi*. A just *thing* (the neuter singular form) is *dikaion*. Just *things* (the neuter plural form) is *dikaia*. Its adverb, justly, is *dikaiōs*. Feminine words tend to have the ending *-ē* (singular) and *-ai* (plural). Thus *aretē* means excellence, while *aretai* means excellences. There are only two main exceptions to this in the text. The plural of *polis* (a city) is *poleis* (cities); *hēdus* (pleasant) has as its neuter singular *hēdu* (a pleasant thing), and as its neuter plural *hēdea* (pleasant things).

Preface

We have followed the Oxford Classical Text. Marginal numbering in the translation refers as closely as possible to that text. We have omitted line numbers to avoid confusion between the translation and the Greek text. Section headings in the translation refer to the sections of the Commentary and are not part of the original text.

As this book is intended principally as an exercise in philosophical thinking and textual exegesis, we have not attempted to provide extensive background information. Where we thought it essential to the reader's understanding, we have incorporated biographical or historical material into the questions in the commentary. Brief details of people referred to in the dialogue have been given in the Biographical index at the end of the commentary. The Index lists mainly Greek words and principal themes, and is intended as a guide to the development of important issues in the dialogue rather than as an *index locorum*. Hence the cited word does not necessarily appear in the listed Commentary question, and the student may need to think through the question as a whole in order to understand the connection.

We suggest that the reader first read a section of the translation, preferably aloud, and then consider the questions for that section by discussing them or by giving written answers. The questions are organised as follows: the Arabic numerals denote major points; successive questions depend on the previous answers. By the end of a section several ideas should have emerged which link the whole section to previous sections, and which anticipate what is to come. Under most Arabic numerals there are sub-questions, indicated by Roman numerals. These either elucidate the main question (which may be difficult to answer on its own), suggest objections to answers which have probably been posed for the main question, or push the reader to consider implications of the direction which the questioning is taking. In short, for the commentary to work, the reader must answer the questions systematically. The natural tendency to cheat, to read right through a section to find out 'what it is getting at' won't work; the final questions of a section will make sense only in the light of earlier an-

Preface

swers. There will certainly be a temptation to rush through
questions which seem to have obvious answers. This too is
a bad practice. We have found that when readers let a
seemingly obvious problem flit by, they cannot, when
pressed, put into words either what the text is about or
what they think about it. We hope to break students of the
habit of uncritical reading by encouraging them to exercise
self-discipline by studying the commentary systematically.

That this commentary-in-questions has affinity with Socrates' own dialectical method is no accident. Nor is the
choice of the *Protagoras*. A central theme of the dialogue,
perhaps the most important, is the conflict between the
passive ingestion and active analysis of what people say.
Protagoras is presented as the masterful purveyor of pat
but elegantly-packaged conventional wisdoms. Socrates is,
as always, the gadfly. But the gadfly is here somewhat
waspish, temperamental, not always on solid ground, in
short, not the totally admirable character of, say, the
Apology or the *Crito*, two dialogues often read by students
new to Plato. This duality in the portrait of Socrates, and
Protagoras' interesting and persuasive, if flawed, arguments make this dialogue the most well-rounded display of
the dialectical method in action that Plato wrote. This is a
conversation among real people, not a near-monologue for
Socrates and a yes-man. It is the archetype of the serious
discussions we find ourselves in from time to time, whether
it be in a formal academic context or in argument with
friends about some current political issue. The near-collapse
of the dialogue a third of the way through, the rapid and
sometimes obscure changes of direction in the debate, the
introduction of seeming irrelevancies, the lengthy excursus
into literary exegesis in the middle – all these make the
Protagoras closer to a piece of theatre, or to a recording of
a real conversation, than to a philosophical set-piece.

But amid these devices of the fiction-writer is a core of
formal logic and philosophy. And yet when we try to ask
what the *Protagoras* is about, no one answer is satisfactory.
The relation to each other of the moral excellences? The
relation of the will to moral judgment (the Socratic Paradox)? Can ethics be taught? Is an ethical system a response

to environmental dictates or to something innate in human beings? Can we learn, can we be taught, to govern our society wisely? How can we judge the competence of a teacher, if the criteria by which we judge him are those which we have come to him to learn? Is this dialogue really a series of experiments in language and logic? Of all Plato's shorter works the *Protagoras* covers most widely the range of moral philosophy which, dealing as it does with issues which are of immediate interest, is perhaps the best introduction to philosophy in general. In addition the logical set-pieces present not only the problems and methods of formal argument, but explore the ways in which fallacious arguments can appear plausible because of ambiguities and equivocations in the terms used to express them.

This book, then, attempts to present to the student this range of topics, always, however, in the belief that in this dialogue, more than in any other, Plato used the figure of Socrates to embody the most important fruit of the real Socrates' life – the realisation that there are rarely clear answers to questions, and that what seems like an answer is only a door to another question.

Among all those who have helped us we want to express our most especial gratitude to I. M. Crombie and David Harvey, whose detailed and painstaking criticism of our manuscript has had a profound influence on the final book. We can only hope that we have done justice to their efforts.

We are grateful for the interest of Profs. W. G. Forrest, M. F. Burnyeat and J. Gould, all of whom saw parts of this book in its early stages and whose comments encouraged us to persevere. In addition others have read the book in its final stages; to all of these we wish to express our appreciation for comments and suggestions: Prof. C. Collard, D. J. Collinson, C. Emlyn-Jones, G. Fallows, Martyn Goff, J. P. Griffin, Prof. Matthew Lipman, Christopher Rowe, and Prof. P. Wiseman. Our thanks goes, as well, to Downside School, to its headmaster Dom Philip Jebb OSB, and to Dom Raphael Appleby OSB, for the help and support they have given to our work.

Downside School   B.A.F.H.
1982   E.S.K.

The Protagoras

Section I*

Friend:	Socrates, where have you appeared from? As if it weren't obvious: you've been on a hunt, haven't you; chasing the youthful Alcibiades? And I certainly did think him a *beautiful* (*kalos*) young man when I saw him the other day; but a man for all that, Socrates, and, strictly between ourselves, already beginning to sprout a beard.	309a
Socrates:	Well, and what of that? Don't you agree with Homer when he says that the most charming age is that of early manhood – the age Alcibiades is now?	b
Friend:	And today? Have you, in fact, been with him? How is the young man disposed towards you?	
Socrates:	Oh, pretty well, I think, and especially today. He spoke up in my defence several times, and indeed I have only just now left him. But actually, I have something rather odd to tell you: though he was there, I paid him no attention and several times I quite forgot about him.	
Friend:	How could such a thing possibly happen between you two? You didn't, I take it, encounter a greater *beauty* in the *city* (*polis*)?	c
Socrates:	Very much so, yes.	
Friend:	What? A citizen or a foreigner?	
Socrates:	A foreigner.	
Friend:	Where from?	
Socrates:	Abdera.	
Friend:	And this foreigner, whoever he is; you found	

* Section headings refer to the Commentary and are not part of the original text.

1

		him so *beautiful* that he actually seemed *fairer* (*kalliōn*) to you than Cleinias' son?
	Socrates:	But my dear fellow, is not the *greatest wisdom* (*to sophōtaton*) likely to be the greater *beauty*?
	Friend:	Then you have come from some *wise man* (*sophos*), Socrates?
d	*Socrates:*	Yes indeed. The wisest of any living, if, that is, you think Protagoras is the wisest.
	Friend:	What's that you say? Protagoras has come to town?
	Socrates:	Two days ago, yes.
	Friend:	And you have just been conversing with him?
310a	*Socrates:*	Indeed so, having said and heard many things.
	Friend:	Well then, why don't you give us the whole story of your conversation? Make this slave give up his seat, and sit down – if you have no other business, that is.
	Socrates:	Certainly: in fact you will be doing me a kindness by listening.
	Friend:	And you us, by giving us the story.
	Socrates:	Then the kindness will be mutual. Well now, listen.

Section II

Early this morning, when it was still pitch dark, Hippocrates, Apollodorus' boy, the brother of Phason, started b hammering at my door with his staff; and when someone opened up, he came rushing straight in and said at the top of his voice: 'Socrates, are you awake or asleep?' And recognising his voice I said: 'Oh, it's Hippocrates. Nothing up, is there?'

'Nothing but good,' he said.

'That,' I said, 'really would be good news. But what is it, and why have you come round at this hour?'

'Protagoras has come,' he said, standing beside me.

'Yes,' I said, 'the day before yesterday. Have you only just found that out?'

c 'Of course,' he said; 'well, yesterday evening, that is.' And

2

Section III

groping for my camp bed, he sat down by my feet and said: 'Yes, in the evening, rather late actually, after I got back from Oenoe. Satyrus, my slave, was on the run, you see, and I was going to tell you that I was after him, when something came up and put it out of my head. And after dinner, when we were off to bed, my brother tells me Protagoras has come. And even then I set out to tell you straight away, but then it occurred to me that it was too late. But as soon as I had slept off my fatigue, I got straight d up and was on my way here, as you see.'

Knowing how bold and volatile he is, I remarked: 'But what has this got to do with you? You don't have some charge to bring against Protagoras, do you?'

'Indeed I do, Socrates,' he laughed: 'that he alone is *wise* (*sophos*), but is not making me wise.'

'Oh yes he will, by Zeus,' I said; 'if you give him money e and persuade him, he will make you wise too.'

'Oh by Zeus and all the gods, if it were just a question of money,' he said, 'I should spare none of my own or my friends' possessions. But that is just what I came to see you about – to get you to talk to him for me. I am rather young, and I have never seen Protagoras before, or ever heard anything he has said. I was still a child when he was last in town. But after all, Socrates, everyone is praising him and saying that he is very *clever* (*sophōtatos*) at speaking. But why don't we go there so that we can catch him in? He 311a is staying with Callias, the son of Hipponicus, so I've heard. Come on.'

And I said: 'Let's not go there yet, my dear fellow; it's still early. Let's get up instead and go out into the courtyard where we can take a few turns until it gets light. Then we can go. After all, Protagoras spends much of his time indoors; so you needn't worry; we shall probably catch him in.

Section III

At this we got up and strolled about the courtyard. And to b put Hippocrates to the test I gave him a searching look and

3

The Protagoras

said: 'Tell me, Hippocrates, you are taking it upon yourself
to go to Protagoras and to pay him a fee on your own behalf
in his capacity as a ... what? With the expectation of becoming ... what? For instance, suppose you have a mind to
go to your namesake, Hippocrates of Cos, the servant of
Asclepius, and to pay him a fee on your own behalf. If
someone were to ask you "Tell me, Hippocrates, you mean
to pay Hippocrates a fee in his capacity as a ... what?",

c what answer would you give?'
'I should say, as a doctor,' he said.
'With a view to becoming ... what?'
'A doctor,' he said.
'Or suppose you intend,' I said, 'to go to Polycleitus of
Argos, or Pheidias of Athens, and pay him a fee on your
own behalf: if someone were to ask "You are intending to
hire Polycleitus or Pheidias as ... what?", what would your
answer be?'
'I should say, as sculptors,' he said.
'With a view to becoming ... what?'
'A sculptor, obviously.'

d 'Well then,' I said, 'we are prepared, you and I, to go to
Protagoras and pay him money on your behalf; and if we
have enough money, to use that to persuade him, or, if that
fails, to use our relatives' money as well. So if, seeing us so
eager, someone should ask us: "Tell me, Socrates and Hippocrates, you are intending to pay Protagoras a fee in his
capacity as a ... what?", what should we reply to him?

e What other name do we hear used of Protagoras? In the
case of Pheidias it is the name of "sculptor", or, in the case
of Homer, the name of "poet". What similar type of name
do we hear applied to Protagoras?'
'Well, a *sophist* (*sophistēs*) is what they call the man,
Socrates.'
'So it is as a sophist then that we are going to pay him
the money?'
'Certainly.'
'Then if someone went on to ask you "And what about

312a you; you are going to Protagoras with a view to becoming
... what?" '
And then, with a blush – for it was just growing light

4

Section IV

enough for me to see him clearly – he said: 'Well, if it is like the other examples, obviously I would expect to become a sophist.'

'But for heaven's sake!' I said, 'wouldn't you be ashamed to make yourself known among the Greeks as a sophist?'

'Yes, of course, Socrates, if I must give my own opinion.'

'But in that case, Hippocrates, perhaps it is not this kind of instruction which you expect from Protagoras, but rather the kind which you received from your instructors in letters or music or athletics? Under each of these you were instructed so that you could acquire not some *skill* (*technē*) or profession, but the kind of liberal education suitable for a free man of independent means.'

'I think instruction under Protagoras is more like that,' he said; 'yes.'

Section IV

Section IV

'Well, do you know what you are about to do, or don't you realise?' I said.

'How do you mean?'

'That you are about to place your own *mind* (*psuchē*) in the care of a man who is, as you say, a sophist; although I should be amazed if you knew just what a sophist might be. And yet if you don't know that, you don't know whether the thing to which you have entrusted your mind is *good* (*agathon*) or *bad* (*kakon*).'

'I think I know,' he said.

'All right, tell me: what do you consider a sophist to be?'

'So far as I am concerned,' he said, 'he is what the word implies: someone who has knowledge of *wise things* (*sopha*).'

'Well, it is possible to say as much of painters and builders, that they have "knowledge of wise things". But should someone ask us "What wise things are painters knowledgeable about?", I suppose we should tell him that it was the production of paintings, and so on. But what if someone were to ask "Yes, but what about the sophist; what wise

5

things is he knowledgeable about?", what would our answer be? In relation to what productive activity is he knowledgeable?'

'What should we say, Socrates? That he knows how to make a man clever at speaking?'

'And our answer might possibly be true, too,' I said, 'but not sufficient. For the answer raises a further question as to what the sophist makes a man clever at speaking about.

e For example, the lyrist presumably makes people clever at speaking on the subject about which he makes them knowledgeable – yes?'

'Yes.'

'Very well, what about the sophist? What does he make people clever at speaking about?'

'Obviously the subject about which he makes them knowledgeable.'

'No doubt. But what is this subject about which, being knowledgeable himself, the sophist makes his student knowledgeable as well?'

'Oh dear,' he said, 'now I have nothing left to say.'

Section V

313a At this I said: 'What's this? You do know what a risk you are about to take with your *mind* (*psuchē*)? If you had to place your body in somebody's care at the risk of its becoming good or bad, you would make a thorough inquiry to establish whether it was advisable or not, and consult the opinions of your friends and relations, and spend several days considering it; but now that something is at stake which you value more highly than your body – your *mind* – by which your entire welfare is determined, depending on whether your mind turns out good or bad – you didn't con-

b sult your father, or your brother, or any of your friends, including me, as to whether you should place your mind in the care of this foreigner who has just arrived, but instead, after hearing of it in the evening, as you tell me, first thing

6

in the morning you turn up, without giving any account of him or asking for any advice about whether you ought to place yourself in his hands or not, and you are ready to spend both your own money and that of your friends, as though you had already arrived at the considered judgment that association with Protagoras was an absolute must, when you neither know him, as you yourself told me, nor have you ever spoken with him before, but you call him a c sophist, and yet, asked what a sophist is, you show manifest ignorance, though you mean to put yourself in his hands.'

'It does rather look like that, Socrates,' he replied 'judging from what you've been saying.'

'Well, Hippocrates, isn't the sophist in reality a sort of merchant or dealer in wares by which the *mind* (*psuchē*) is fed? Certainly he seems to me to be something of the kind.'

'Yes, but by what is a mind fed, Socrates?'

'By *learning* (*mathēmata*), presumably,' I said. 'And take care, my friend, that the sophist doesn't take us in with his advertisements as do the merchant and dealer in food for the body. For they too do not know which of the wares they d peddle are good for the body and which bad, any more than their customers do – unless one of them happens to be an expert in physical fitness or medicine. And yet they promote all their wares equally. The same applies to those who hawk their *courses of instruction* (*mathēmata*) round the various cities, flogging them to anyone who happens to want them; they give equal promotion to everything they have for sale, though it may well be the case, my excellent friend, that some of these men also do not know which of their wares are good for the mind and which bad, unless one of them happens to be an expert in the care of the mind; and the e same holds true for their customers. So in your case, if you happen to know which of these courses of instruction are good for the mind and which bad, you can safely purchase them from Protagoras or from anyone you please. But if not, beware, my dear boy; you may be dicing with your dearest possession. In fact, where the purchase of *instruction* (*math-* 314a *ēmata*) is concerned, the danger is much greater. For when we buy food and drink from a dealer or merchant, we can take them away in other containers and, before we allow

7

them to enter our system by eating or drinking them, we can take them home, put them away and take the advice of an expert as to which we should eat or drink and which we should not, and in what quantities and upon what occasions,
b   so that the purchase itself carries no great risk. But with a course of instruction we cannot take it away in any other container, but are compelled to put down our money and go away after we have *learned* (*manthanein*) and let the course enter our very mind, whether to its benefit or detriment. So let's examine these courses and take the advice of our elders, for we are still a little young to exercise discretion over such an important issue. All the same, let's go now, as we planned, and listen to the man. Then, after we have heard him let's join the company of some others. After all, Prota-
c   goras isn't the only one there, but Hippias of Elis as well, and Prodicus of Ceos too, I think, and many other wise men.'

Section VI

This agreed, we set off; but when we reached the porch we stayed a while, continuing a discussion which had arisen between us on our way. So, preferring to complete it before going in, rather than break off in the middle, we continued our conversation in the porch until we arrived at a mutually acceptable conclusion. And I suppose the doorman, a eun-
d   uch, must have been listening to us; and what with the number of sophists in the house and the resulting stream of visitors, I fear he was fed up. At all events, when we knocked he opened the door, took one look at us and said 'Huh! Sophists! Master's busy', and promptly used both his hands to slam the door as hard as he could.

We knocked again and he answered through the door – locked by now.

'Hey, you,' he said, 'didn't you hear me say Master's busy?'

'But my good fellow,' I said, 'we haven't come to see Cal-
e   lias. And we aren't sophists either – don't worry. It's Protagoras we've come to see, so show us in.' And at last the

man grudgingly opened the door.

We entered to find Protagoras walking up and down the portico, while walking up and down with him were, in order, on one side Callias the son of Hipponicus, his maternal step-brother Paralus the son of Pericles, and Charmides the   315a
son of Glaucon, and, on the other side, Pericles' other son Xanthippus, Philippides the son of Philomelus and Anti-moerus of Mende, who is Protagoras' star pupil and is study-ing to acquire the art and become a sophist. And of those who followed behind, listening in on their discourse, the majority seemed to be foreigners. Protagoras draws these people from every city he visits, enchanting them, like Or-   b
pheus, with his voice, while they follow after his voice spell-bound. But there were also a few native Athenians in the chorus. I particularly enjoyed the spectacle of this chorus and the splendid care they took never to be in Protagoras' way or get in front of him. Each time he and his companions turned about, his audience parted ranks in good order, this way and that, and so, circling about, returned each time to their positions in the rear: magnificent!

'After him I beheld' (as Homer says) Hippias of Elis seated   c
in state in the portico opposite, while about him, on benches, sat Eryximachus the son of Acumenus, Phaedrus the Myr-rhinusan and Andron the son of Androtion, together with some foreigners from his own native city, and some others. As it appeared, they were plying Hippias with questions about natural science and astronomy while he, from his chair of state, was deciding any arguments which arose and giving lengthy expositions in answer to their questions.

'Tantalus then I espied' (as Homer also says); for Prodicus   d
of Ceos was in town as well. He was in a chamber which Hipponicus had previously used as a storeroom; but because of the number of guests, Callias had cleared this room out and turned it into a guest-room for his visitors. Anyway, Prodicus was still in bed, wrapped in sheepskins and blan-kets – a considerable quantity, to judge from his appear-ance. Sitting beside him on the nearby couches were Pausanias from Cerameis, and with Pausanias a young stri-pling, of good breeding, I think, and extremely good looking. I heard his name as Agathon, I think, and I shouldn't be   e

9

surprised if he isn't actually Pausanias' boyfriend. Anyway, there was this lad, the two Adeimantuses, one the son of Cepis and the other the son of Leucolophides, and apparently some others. But from where I was standing, outside, I was unable to discover what they were discussing, though I was eager to hear Prodicus. For I think he is a very wise man indeed – wonderfully so. But his voice was so deep that the reverberation of the room made his words indistinct.

316a

We had only just come in when behind us came Alcibiades – the beautiful, as you call him, and I agree – together with Critias the son of Callaeschrus.

Section VII

So we came on in. But still we hung back a little while, taking in the scene before us. Then we went up to Protagoras.

b

'Excuse me, Protagoras,' I said. 'Hippocrates here and I have come to see you.'

'Do you want to speak with me in private,' he said, 'or in front of the others?'

'So far as we are concerned,' I said, 'it makes no difference. You can decide for yourself when you have heard the purpose of our visit.'

'Well,' he said, 'what is the purpose of your visit?'

'Hippocrates here is a native of this town. His father is Apollodorus and he comes from an important and prosperous family. He is, moreover, temperamentally disposed to compete with other young men of his age, and I think he desires a name in the *community* (*polis*). This he thinks he would be most likely to achieve by associating himself with you. So now with this in mind, decide whether you prefer to discuss all this in private or in front of the others.'

c

'Your consideration for me is very proper, Socrates,' he said. 'For when a man visits great *cities* (*poleis*) as a foreigner, and in those cities persuades the best of their young men to forsake the company of all others, whether of family

10

or of friends, old or young, and to associate with him alone, expecting by that very association to become better men – when, I say, a man is engaged in such activities, he must take precautions. For this kind of activity causes considerable unpopularity and even a variety of malicious conspiracies. However, I myself declare that the sophistic *art* (*technē*) itself has a long-standing tradition, whereas its practitioners in former times were intimidated by its unpopularity, and therefore concealed it behind specious façades. Thus there are some, like Homer, Hesiod or Simonides, who have hidden it behind a façade of poetry, while others made use of mystery cults or prophecy, as did the Orphics and the followers of Musaeus. Similarly I have perceived some such use of physical training: Iccus of Taras, for example, and even today Herodicus of Selymbria, formerly of Megara, is as able a sophist as any. Then there was your own Agathocles who presented himself to the public as a practitioner of music, though he was in fact a great sophist, and Pythocleides of Ceos and many more besides. All these men, I say, fearing unpopularity, used these *arts* as window-dressing. But I differ from all of them. I consider that they failed to accomplish their objective: for they did not pass undetected by those men who played a leading part in their *communities*, and for whose benefit they put up these façades in the first place; after all, the *masses* (*polloi*) notice hardly anything for themselves, merely acclaiming whatever these leading citizens pronounce. For a man to run for cover, and not only to fail to get away but actually to make himself conspicuous in the process is in itself sheer stupidity; besides which it will inevitably make people even more hostile, since they regard that sort of man as unprincipled into the bargain. Which is why I have taken precisely the opposite course from these men and openly admit to being a sophist and an educator, thinking it a better precaution to admit to it openly than to be caught denying it. And in addition to this I have taken other precautions which, with the help of God, ensure that I can openly admit, without any unpleasant consequences, that I am a sophist. And yet I have been practising the art for many years now; indeed I have been alive for a great many years – indeed,

d

e

317a

b

c

11

I am old enough to be the father of any one of you. So if there is something you want, much the most agreeable course for me would be to talk it over in front of all the other visitors to this house.'

Now I had a suspicion that he wanted to show off to Prodicus and Hippias, and parade the fact that the new

d arrivals were admirers of his. So I said: 'Well then, why don't we call Prodicus and Hippias and their companions? They can listen in on our conversation as well.'

'Certainly,' said Protagoras.

'Do you want us to arrange the seating in a circle so that you can be seated for your conversation?' said Callias. It was agreed, and in our eagerness to hear these *wise men* (*sophoi*) we all set to and actually shifted the benches and sofas ourselves, arranging them by Hippias as the benches were already over there. Meanwhile Callias and Alcibiades

e brought Prodicus over with his companions, after helping him up off his bed.

Section VIII

When we were all assembled Protagoras began: 'Now, Socrates, perhaps you could repeat, for the benefit of these people here, the matter which you outlined to me just now on behalf of the young man.'

318a   And I said: 'I shall begin as before, Protagoras, with my reason for coming. It so happens that Hippocrates here desires to associate with you. So he wishes to learn what, if he does associate with you, the outcome of his studies will be. That is all we have to say.'

'If you associate with me, young man,' said Protagoras in reply, 'then you will be able, at the end of your first day in my company, to go away a better man; and the same will happen on the next day, and each day after that you will continue to grow better and improve.'

b   At this I said: 'There is nothing surprising in what you say so far, Protagoras; in fact it is what I should expect.

12

Section VIII

Even in your case, despite your seniority and wisdom, were someone to give you instruction on a subject about which, by some chance, you knew nothing, you too would grow better. But that is not what I meant. Think of it this way: suppose Hippocrates here were suddenly to change his mind and set his heart on associating with that young man who is in town at the moment – Zeuxippus, from Heraclea, I mean – and came to him, just as he has come to you, and c heard him say just what he has heard from you: that each day on which he associates with him he will grow better and make progress; and suppose someone were to ask Zeuxippus the further question, "At what are you saying he will grow better, and towards what will he make progress?", Zeuxippus would say at painting. Or suppose that in company with Orthagoras of Thebes he heard what he has heard from you, and were again to ask at what he would be better each day by his association with him; he would say at playing the flute. Well, in the same way, Protagoras, tell the young lad and me (since I am asking the question on his behalf) the following: If Hippocrates here associates with d Protagoras, he will go away better on the first day and will make progress every day after that – but towards what, Protagoras, and in relation to what?'

'You ask a good question, Socrates,' said Protagoras, hearing me say this, 'and I'm always pleased to reply to a good question. If Hippocrates comes to me he won't have the same experience as he would have had by associating with one of the other sophists. These others are a curse on young men. Just when they have escaped from *technical subjects* e (*technai*), they bring them unwillingly back and throw them once again into technical subjects – arithmetic, astronomy, geometry, music' – this with a pointed look at Hippias – 'but with me he will learn only the subject which he came to learn and no other. The course of instruction is *good planning (euboulia)* both of his own affairs, to the end that he would best manage his personal estate, and of the *city's* 319a (*polis*), to the end that he would be in the strongest position to conduct, in speech and action, the common business of the city.'

'Am I following you correctly?' I said. 'It seems to me that

13

the technical subject of which you speak is *citycraft (politikē techne)*, and that you are promising to make men *good members of their city (agathoi politai).'*

'That, Socrates,' he said, 'is precisely the declaration which I am making.'

Section IX

'Well,' I said, 'this is a fine *technique (technēma)* you have acquired, if indeed you have acquired it. For you will get from me nothing less than my honest opinion. That is, Protagoras, I didn't think that this was something which could be taught. But now that you say it is, I don't know what to
b do but take your word for it. Still, it's only right that I should say why I do consider that it can be neither taught nor passed on by one man to another. You see, I, in common with all other Greeks, call the Athenians *wise (sophoi)*. And I observe that whenever we convene in the *assembly (ekklēsia)*, and the city has some business related to building, it is the builders who are summoned as *advisers (sumbouloi)* about the buildings; or again, if ship construction is involved, it is the shipwrights, and the same for every other matter which they consider is capable of being both learnt
c and taught. And if someone else attempts *to give them advice (sumbouleuein)*, whom they don't consider a skilled professional, be he *handsome (kalos)* and wealthy and well-born, they will have none of him, for all that, but laugh and jeer at him until this man who has ventured to speak either stands down of his own accord, discouraged by the uproar, or is dragged from the platform by the police or removed on the order of the presidents. That is what they do when they consider a *technical skill (technē)* to be at issue. But when they come *to deliberate (bouleuesthai)* poli-
d tical issues, then a builder can get up and *give advice (sumbouleuein)*, or, equally, smith or cobbler, merchant or shipper, rich or poor, high-born or low, without distinction. And nobody heckles them, as they do in the previous instances, with shouts of "You didn't learn about it anywhere. No

qualified instructor trained you, and now you try to give us advice!'". And the reason is plainly that they don't consider that it can be taught.

'But it isn't just that the common affairs of the city are conducted like that. Even in private life our best and wisest   e citizens are unable to pass on this *excellence (aretē)* to others. Take Pericles, the father of these two young men here. In all the fields which fall within the competence of teachers, he has had them excellently educated. But in the   320a one field in which he is himself *wise (sophos)*, he neither educates them himself nor does he put them in someone else's hands. No, he lets them roam free, like sacred flocks, in the hope that they will somehow stumble upon this excellence of their own accord. Or take Cleinias, if you like, the younger brother of Alcibiades here. This same man, Pericles, is his guardian, and he was concerned that Alcibiades might have a corrupting influence upon him. So he dragged him away from the company of Alcibiades, and placed him in Ariphon's household to be educated. But not six months had passed before he returned him to his brother, not knowing what to do with him. And there are   b many others I could cite who, for all their good qualities, have never yet made anyone better, be it their own or anyone else's sons. It is with this in view, Protagoras, that I don't consider that *excellence* can be taught. But when I hear the suggestion coming from you, I begin to have second thoughts and to think that you must have a point, since I consider you to be a man of wide experience who has acquired extensive knowledge both from learning and from your own researches. If, therefore, you can give us a clearer demonstration that excellence can be taught, please don't   c stint us, but give give a demonstration.'

'Of course I shan't stint you, Socrates,' he said. 'But shall I present my demonstration in the manner of an elder to younger men, by telling a story, or shall I expound an argument?'

Several of the assembled company interrupted and told him to use whichever method he pleased.

'In that case,' said Protagoras, 'I think it will be more congenial if I tell you a story.'

15

The Protagoras
Section X (XI)*

'There once was a time when there were gods, but no mortal
d   creatures. And when the time came which was decreed by
fate for their creation also, the gods figured them within the
earth, compounding them of earth and of fire, and of everything which is mixed with fire and earth. And when they
were ready to lead them towards the light, they charged
Prometheus and Epimetheus that they should furnish and
distribute powers to each as it should be fitting. But Epimetheus begged Prometheus and asked that he might himself make distribution, saying "Let me first distribute;
afterward examine my work". And when he had persuaded
him with these words he began to make distribution. And
as he distributed, to some he added strength without speed,
while the weaker he furnished with swiftness. And some he
e   armed, while to others he gave an unarmed nature, devising
for them instead some other power for their safety. For
whichsoever he confined and made small of stature, to these
he distributed a refuge of wings or a dwelling under the
earth; but whichsoever he made great of stature, by their
321a very greatness he kept them safe. And so, in like manner,
he made just and equal distribution, devising these things
as a precaution lest any kind might vanish from the earth.
'But when for each he had prepared a refuge from the
others against destruction, next he devised comfort against
the seasons sent by Zeus, clothing them about with thick
fur and tough hide sufficient to keep out the winter and
able to resist the scorching sun, and in order also that when
they took themselves to their rest, these things might sup-
ply to each its own natural covering for the night. And some
b   he shod with hooves, and others with tough and bloodless
hide. Next he supplied for them varied nourishment – to
some the plants of the earth, to others the fruit of trees, and

* Protagoras' entire speech is discussed in Section X of the commentary.
Section XI of the commentary deals with the story only (320c–323a); XII
deals with the remainder of the speech (323a–328d). Section X is therefore
wholly comprised of XI and XII. The creation myth is told in a distinct,
somewhat archaic style reminiscent of the manner of Herodotus or even
Hesiod. We have sought to highlight this change of style by reverting to
a reminiscence of Biblical prose, even at the risk of exaggerating a little
the archaic effect.

16

Section X (XI)

to others roots. And to some he granted other creatures for their sustenance, adding to these meagreness of progeny, but to their prey abundant fruitfulness, supplying their kind with a means for their preservation.

'But because Epimetheus was not exceeding wise, he exhausted all the powers upon the brute beasts and noticed it not. Yet still humankind was left unfurnished, so that he   c
was perplexed what he should do. And being thus perplexed behold there came to him Prometheus to examine his distribution. And he found the other animals diligently provided for, but man without clothing, without shoes, without coverings for the night, without weapons. And already the allotted day was at hand in which man must come out of the earth into the light. Being thus sore perplexed as to what safety he should find for man, Prometheus stole from   d
Hephaestus and Athene *practical wisdom* (*entechnē sophia*) together with fire – for without fire no man may acquire or make use of this – and he bestowed them upon man. In this way man acquired *wisdom* for his sustenance, but he did not have *citycraft*. For it lay with Zeus. Nor was it any longer permitted to Prometheus to approach the citadel where Zeus had his habitation; and moreover the guardians of Zeus were fearsome. But he came in stealth to the common habitation of Hephaestus and Athene, in which they practised their *skill* (*technē*), and stealing the *skills* of He-   e
phaestus – which is working with fire – and of Athene, he gave them to men, so that it came to pass that man had abundant means for his sustenance. Afterward Prometheus   322a
was charged with theft, as it is told, because of Epimetheus.

'Since there was a part of man which was divine, he alone of all living things began, because of his kinship with the gods, to believe in gods and to build altars and images of gods. And then soon, by his skill, he began to speak and to use words; he invented dwellings and clothing and shoes, coverings for the night and nourishment from the earth. Being thus equipped, men were scattered at the beginning, and there were no cities, so that they were destroyed by   b
wild animals because they were weaker in all things. And though the skill of their hands was sufficient for their sustenance, for warring against the beasts it was not sufficient.

17

For they did not yet have *citycraft*, of which *warcraft* (*polemikē technē*) is a part. At first they sought to gather together for their safety by founding cities. But when they were gathered together, they *committed injury* (*adikein*) one upon another, since they had not the skill of citycraft, so that they were scattered anew and began once more to perish. Whereupon Zeus, being afraid concerning our kind, that it might perish utterly, sent Hermes unto mankind with *justice* (*dikē*) and a *sense of shame* (*aidōs*), to bring order to their cities and common bonds of amity. And Hermes asked Zeus in what manner he ought to give justice and a sense of shame to men, saying: "Am I to distribute them even as the practical skills have been distributed? For thus have they been distributed: one man skilled in medicine is sufficient unto many who have not the skill, as it is also with other men of skill. Am I in like manner to distribute justice and a sense of shame among men, or am I to distribute among all?" "Among all," Zeus replied, "and let all have them in common. For there could be no cities if but a few had them, as it is with the other skills. And lay down this law from me: if any man be not able to share justice and a sense of shame even as other men do, they must kill him as a pestilence to the city."

'That, Socrates, is why the Athenians – as indeed everyone else – hold the view that when their deliberations require excellence at building and other such practical skills, only a restricted group of men should contribute advice, and so they refuse to tolerate advice from anyone outside that group, as you say (naturally so, I would add); and that is why, on the contrary, when their deliberations involve *political excellence* (*politikē aretē*), and must be conducted entirely on the basis of *justice* (*dikaiosunē*) and *moderation* (*sōphrosunē*) they quite naturally tolerate everyone. For they believe that all men must have this excellence in common, since otherwise there could be no *cities* (*poleis*). That is the reason for this, Socrates.

Section X (XII)

'And in case you should think I am deceiving you when I say that all men really do believe that *justice*, along with the rest of *political excellence*, is something which every single individual has in common, here is further evidence. In the case of the other excellences it is true, as you say, that if someone claims to be good at some such *skill* as flute-playing when in fact he isn't, people treat him with derision or annoyance, while his family and friends take him on one side and warn him that he is out of his mind; but where justice and the rest of political excellence is concerned, if a man truthfully accuses himself in public of being *unjust* (*adikos*), even in cases where he is actually known to be *unjust*, then that very truthfulness, which in the former case was regarded as *moderation*, in this case they treat as madness, and say that everyone should claim to be *just* (*dikaios*), whether he is or not, and that the man who doesn't put up some show of being just is out of his mind, in the belief that no one can fail to have at least some share of justice, or he would not be human.

'So much, then, for my claim that it is natural for them to recognise all men as competent to give advice on questions related to this excellence, in consequence of their belief that all men have it in common. That they consider it to be a teachable thing possessed in every case as a result rather of teaching and practice than of chance or birth, I shall now try to show. Where a man's failings are thought to be the result of chance or birth, he doesn't become the object of anger, admonition, correction or punishment, nor of any attempt to alter him. He is the object, rather, of pity. Who, for example, would be so foolish as to attempt any such thing with the ugly or small or puny? For men know, I think, that such things as beauty and its opposite are due either to birth or to chance. But when it comes to those human excellences which are generally regarded as the products of training or practice or teaching, if someone lacks these and has the opposite failings, why then it is that anger, punishment and admonition are brought into play; and among these failings are *injustice* (*adikia*), impiety and,

b

c

d

e

19

324a all in all, the complete opposite of *political excellence*. Where men grow angry with one another and admonish one another, it is clear that they do so in the belief that this is an excellence which can be acquired by practice and instruction. For consider, if you will, Socrates, the influence of punishment upon those who *commit injustice (adikein)*, and the institution itself will show you that men regard excellence as something which can be acquired. For no one punishes anyone because of the mere fact that he has committed an injustice and with that alone in mind, unless he is inflicting unreasoned punishment as one might upon a brute

b beast. No, the man who exacts reasoned punishment does so not because of the past injustice – the past cannot be undone – but for the sake of the future: to deter him, or another who sees him punished, from committing a further injustice. And since he has this belief, it follows that he believes that excellence can be inculcated; deterrence is, after all, his purpose in inflicting punishment. This, then, is the opinion of all those who impose punishment, whether

c on their own or on the city's account; punishment and correction are in fact imposed by all men, and foremost among them the Athenians, your fellow-citizens, upon those they believe guilty of injustice. It follows, therefore, on this argument, that the Athenians are also among those who believe that excellence is something which can be inculcated and taught. So, Socrates, you have had a sufficient demonstration, as it seems to me, that it is quite natural for your fellow-citizens to recognize both smith and cobbler as competent to give advice on political questions, and that they take the view that excellence can be taught and acquired.

d 'There remains the difficulty you experience in relation to good men, as to why it might be that in subjects which are the province of teachers, they teach their own sons and make them *wise*, while at that very excellence in which they are themselves outstanding, they make them no better than anyone else. For this question I shall dispense with parables, Socrates, and give you an argument. Consider: Is there or is there not some single thing which all citizens

e must possess if a city is to exist at all? In this question alone lies the solution to your difficulty. For if there is, and if this

Section X (XII)

single thing is not skill at building or metalwork or pottery, but *justice*, *moderation*, being *holy* (*hosios*) or, in short, what 325a I call manly *excellence*; if this is the excellence which all men must have in common; and if every man, whatever else he wishes to learn or to do, must act in accordance with it and must not act without it, since otherwise whoever lacks it, whether child, man or woman, must either be taught or punished until he improves under punishment, while whoever refuses to respond to punishment and instruction, being regarded as incurable, must be expelled from his city or killed; if all this is so, and if, given that that is its nature, b good men teach their sons every subject but this one, think what strange creatures good men must be. For we have already shown that they think it can be taught in both its public and its private aspects; yet although it can be taught and nurtured, all those other subjects, of which their sons can afford to be ignorant without incurring the death penalty they teach them; but when it comes to the very subject which may bring execution or exile upon their sons if they aren't educated and brought up to excellence, and in c addition to execution the confiscation of their property and, in short, the total ruin of their households, are we then to say that they fail to teach it and don't, on the contrary, devote to it every care? Of course they do, Socrates. They both teach and admonish them from their earliest childhood throughout their whole lives. As soon as the infant can understand what is said to it, nurse, mother, tutor and father himself vie with each other to ensure that the child d will develop the best possible character, so that, whatever it does or says, they instruct it, pointing out that "this is just, that is unjust; this is *fine* (*kalon*), that is *base* (*aischron*); this is holy, that is unholy; do this, don't do that." And if he shows a ready obedience, well and good; if not, then like a warped and twisted plank they straighten him with threats and blows. Next, when they send him to school, they are much more insistent that his teachers should pay attention to the children's seemly conduct than to the lyre and to the alphabet. So the teachers see to this, and when, e in turn, the children have learned their letters and are beginning to understand the written, as before the spoken,

21

326a word, they seat them on benches and set them the works of good poets to read and learn by heart, works containing much good advice, stories, and praises and eulogies of good men of old, so that the child may eagerly imitate and strive to be like such men. Then again the lyre-teachers cultivate in them *self-discipline* (*sōphrosunē*), and ensure that young men do not go wrong in this respect. Moreover, once they have learned to play the lyre, their tutors teach them

b the works of good lyric poets, to the accompaniment of the lyre, and mould the minds of the children to their rhythms and melodies so that, by becoming more calm, graceful and harmonious, they may acquire more facility both of speech and action: for rhythm and harmony are essential to every aspect of a man's life. And then, in addition to all this, they send them to the trainer so that they can have a better

c physique to put at the service of their good character, and not be forced to act like a coward, whether in war or any other enterprise, because they are in poor physical condition.

'And this is done above all by those in the best position to do so – the very rich. They send their sons to school earliest in childhood and keep them under instruction longest. Moreover, when children are released from schooling, the city compels them to learn the *laws* (*nomoi*), and to model their lives on them, so that they may not follow the

d random dictates of personal inclination, but, just as the writing instructor guides those children who aren't yet good at writing by drawing lines with the pen and then handing the slate to the pupil and making him follow the guidance of the lines, so the city gives laws, which were invented by good lawgivers of olden times, as outlines, and compels him to govern and be governed in accordance with these, while it punishes anyone who strays outside them. And this pun-

e ishment, both in your city and in many others besides, has the name "correction", since justice corrects. Given, then, that both individuals and the state as a whole take such pains over excellence, are you really surprised or puzzled that it should be teachable, Socrates? There is no need for surprise: it would be far more surprising if it were not teachable.

22

Section X (XII)

'Why is it, then, that many good fathers have good-for-
nothing sons? Let me explain this too. There is nothing
strange, if I was correct in my previous claim that in this
thing – excellence, that is – no one must be a layman if a   327a
city is to exist at all. For if it is as I say – as it most
assuredly is – consider any other pursuit or study you
choose. If a city couldn't exist unless we are all, say, flute-
players to the best of our abilities, and if everyone taught
each other both in private and public life, using reproof
against incompetent players instead of keeping the skill to
themselves, just as today no one makes a jealously guarded
secret of the just and the *lawful* (*nomima*) as they do with   b
the other skills – because, I think, the justice and excellence
of our relations with each other profits us: which is why we
are all so eager to argue and expound our views on issues
of justice and the law; if, in short, we exhibited the same
total and unstinting enthusiasm for mutual instruction in
flute-playing, do you think, Socrates,' he said, 'that the sons
of good flute-players would show any greater tendency to
become good flute-players than the sons of the incompetent?
I think not. Rather it would be the son most naturally gifted
at flute-playing, irrespective of his origins, who would grow
up to acquire a great reputation, while the ungifted would,
irrespective of his origins, remain unknown. As it is, it   c
frequently happens that the son of a good flute-player turns
out to be useless, while the son of a useless player turns out
to be good. Even so, they would all be good enough perform-
ers in comparison with laymen and those with no knowledge
of the flute whatever. Similarly in our present case, take
whomsoever you consider to be the most unjust of those who
are brought up in the society of men with *laws* (*nomoi*) and
you would find him just and expert in this matter, if you
had to judge him by comparison with men who have neither
education nor *law-courts* (*dikastēria*) nor *laws* nor any com-   d
pulsion of any kind to make them care consistently for
excellence – men like the savages which the poet Pherecrates presented last year at the Lenaea. If you found yourself among such men as the man-haters in that chorus, then
you would be delighted to fall in with Eurybatus or Phrynondas, and would moan with misery and long for the vi-

23

e ciousness of your fellow men here. As it is, you are spoiled, Socrates: because each and every man teaches excellence as well as he is able, you think that no one does. Yet no more would you find one man who teaches people to speak their

328a native Greek, if you were to look for one. No more would you succeed, if you were to try to establish which individual man teaches the sons of our craftsmen, when they have learned from their fathers and from their fathers' fellow-craftsmen all teaching as well as they are able. I do not think it is easy, Socrates,to single out any one of these as the teacher, though it is quite easy to identify their teachers as a group from among the whole populace. And such is the case with excellence and with everything else.

'So that if any one of us is even marginally better at advancing people along the path to excellence, he should be

b welcomed. I believe that I am one of these, being better than others at helping men on their way to becoming *noble and excellent (kaloi k'agathoi)*, worthy of my fee, if not more, as my pupils agree. That is why I have adopted the following method of charging. Any student may, if he wishes, pay me

c my fee in cash. But if not, he can go to a temple, make a sworn declaration of what he believes to be the true value of my instruction, and deposit that sum.

'There now, Socrates,' he said, 'I have given you both parable and argument. I have shown you that excellence can be taught, that the Athenians believe it to be so, and that it isn't surprising that the sons of good fathers turn out to be good-for-nothings – after all, even the sons of Polycleitus, who are contemporaries of Paralus and Xanthippus here, bear no comparison with their father, any more than the sons of other craftsmen do; but it is still too early to find

d fault with them over this; there is still hope for them: for they are young.'

Section XIII

Such was Protagoras' demonstration which he now brought to an end. And for a long time I went on gazing at him,

Section XIII

mesmerised, expecting him to continue, hanging on his words. But when I realised that he really had finished, I recovered, with some difficulty, my presence of mind, and turned to speak to Hippocrates:

'Son of Apollodorus, I thank you most sincerely for having prevailed upon me to come here. To have heard what I have just heard from Protagoras has been invaluable to me. For till now I had been of the opinion that it was not by any human effort that *good men* (*agathoi*) become good. But now he has convinced me.

'Except, that is, for one small difficulty which I am sure Protagoras will easily explain, now that he has already explained so many other points. For indeed, if you went and discussed these very matters with one of our political orators, be it Pericles or another of our competent speakers, you might hear much the same arguments from them. Yet if one of these is asked a further question, they are like books, incapable of returning an answer or asking a question; ask them the slightest question about what they have said and just as bronze vessels, once struck, ring on and on till someone puts a hand to them, so orators, asked the smallest question, spin out a marathon speech. But Protagoras here is equally competent at delivering long and splendid speeches, as we have heard for ourselves, and at answering a question briefly, and, when he has asked a question himself, at waiting to hear other people's replies – a rare attainment.

'So now, Protagoras, I shall have all I need if you would answer me just this. You say that excellence can be taught, and you of all men should be able to convince me. But one thing you said I found strange, and I should like you to satisfy my mind on the point. You were saying that Zeus sent *justice* (*dikaiosunē*) and a sense of shame to man, and again at several points in your speech you were speaking of *justice* and *moderation* (*sōphrosunē*) and *holiness* (*hosiotēs*) and so on, as though they amounted to a single thing: *excellence* (*aretē*). This is the point on which I need a precise explanation. Is it the case that excellence is some single thing, while justice, moderation and holiness are parts of it, or is it that all these things which I mentioned just now are

e

329a

b

c

25

The Protagoras

d names for one and the same single thing? That is what I still need from you.'

'Well, that is an easy question to answer, Socrates,' he said. 'Excellence is a single thing, and the things about which you ask are parts of it.'

'Do you mean,' I said, 'as the parts of the face – mouth, nose, eyes and ears – are parts, or are they like the parts of a lump of gold, indistinguishable from each other and from the whole except in size?'

e 'The former, I think, Socrates. They are related to excellence as the parts of the face are related to the whole face.'

'In that case,' said I 'is it also true that, when men come to have these parts of excellence in common, some have one part and others another, or is it that if a man acquires one he has them all?'

'Certainly not,' he said. 'Many men are *courageous* (*andreioi*) but *unjust*; and many are *just* but not *wise*.'

'So these are also parts of excellence,' I said, '*wisdom* (*sophia*), I mean, and *courage* (*andreia*)?'

330a 'Oh, most certainly so,' he said. 'And wisdom is the greatest of all the parts.'

'And in each case one part is one thing and another is something distinct?'

'Yes.'

'And is it the case that each of them has a unique capacity? Take, for example, the parts of the face: the eye isn't the same kind of thing as the ears, nor does it have the same capacity; nor is any one of the other parts the same kind of thing as any other part, either in its capacity or in any other respect. Is this also true of the parts of excellence; and is it the case that no one part is the same kind of thing b as another part, either in itself or in its capacity? It must be, musn't it, if it conforms to the analogy?'

'It is indeed so, Socrates,' he said. And I said:

'So none of the other parts of excellence is the same kind of thing as *knowledge* (*epistēmē*), and similarly for *justice* (*dikaiosunē*), for *courage* (*andreia*), for *moderation*, (*sōphrosunē*), and for *holiness* (*hosiotēs*)?'

He agreed.

26

Section XIV

'Well, now,' I said, 'let us examine together what kind of thing each of them is, beginning with this. Is *justice* some thing or no thing at all? I think it is; what about you?' c
'I think so too,' he said.
'Very well. Then if someone were to ask me and you "Tell me, Protagoras and Socrates, this thing, as you just termed it, justice: is it itself *just (dikaion)* or *unjust (adikon)*?", my reply would be that it is just. Which way would you vote: the same as me, or otherwise?'
'The same,' he said.
'Then in answer to the question, I should say that justice is a just kind of thing; wouldn't you?' d
'Yes,' he said.
'So that if he should then ask "Don't you also say that holiness is something?" I assume we should say yes.'
'Yes,' he said.
'And if he added "And don't you agree that this also is a thing?" we should say yes, shouldn't we?'
He agreed to this as well.
' "But do you say that the thing itself is essentially an *unholy (anhosion)* kind of thing, or a *holy (hosion)* kind of thing?" For myself I should be indignant and say: "Mortal, guard thy tongue! There could hardly be anything else which is holy if holiness itself is not holy." What about you? e
I take it you would give the same answer?'
'Absolutely,' he said.
'Then if he went on to ask us: "But what was it you were claiming a moment ago? I suppose I heard you correctly? I thought you were saying that the parts of excellence are so related that no one of them can be the same kind of thing as any other." For my part, I should say: "You heard quite correctly, except for your impression that it was I who said it; here you misheard. It was Protagoras here who was making the statement, in reply to my questions." If he were 331a
to respond by saying: "Is it true what this man says, Protagoras? Do you in fact maintain that no part of excellence is the same kind of thing as any other? Is this indeed your position?" How would you reply?'

The Protagoras

'I should have to agree, Socrates,' he said.

'And now that we are agreed on this point, Protagoras, what shall we say if he persists with his questions and says: "So holiness is not a just kind of thing, nor justice a holy kind of thing, but rather of such a kind as not to be holy; while holiness is of such a kind as not to be just, but, in
b   consequence, unjust, and justice unholy"? How should we reply? For if I were to speak for myself, I should say both that justice is holy and that holiness is just; indeed, I should give the same reply on your behalf as well, if you would permit it: that is, that justice is the same as holiness, or as similar as it can be, and above all that justice is the same kind of thing as holiness, and *vice versa*. But consider whether you would prevent me from making this reply for you, or whether you share the same view.'

'Not exactly, Socrates,' he said. I don't think it is just a
c   simple matter of agreeing that justice is holy and holiness just. I think there is a difference there. Still, what does it matter?' he said. 'If you like, we can take it that justice is holy and holiness just.'

'Oh no I can't,' I said; 'it isn't this "if you like" or "if you think so" I want to examine, but me and you. I say "me and you" because I believe that the question will best be examined without the "if".'

d   'Very well,' he said, 'there is a certain similarity between justice and holiness; indeed there could be a certain similarity between anything and virtually anything else. There could be, for example, a certain similarity between black and white, or hard and soft, and so on; though one would say that they were absolute opposites. Thus to return to the previous point, that the parts of the face have each a distinct capacity, and that no one of them is the same kind of thing as any other, there is, nevertheless, a sense in which they are alike and in which one is like another. So by this method
e   you could, if you chose, maintain that they are all alike. But it isn't fair to call things similar merely on the grounds that they bear some one point of similarity, however minor, any more than it is fair to call them dissimilar merely because they have some single dissimilarity.'

Surprised at this, I said: 'Oh, is that how you see the

relationship between justice and holiness – as having only
a minor similarity?'

'Not quite that,' he said, 'but not as you seem to suppose,   332a
either.'

Section XV

'Never mind,' I said; 'since you appear to be unhappy with
that line of argument, let's leave it there and examine one
of your other points. Is there something which you call *folly*
(*aphrosunē*)?'

He assented to this.

'And isn't the absolute opposite of this thing *wisdom*
(*sophia*)?'

'So I believe,' he said.

'Now when men act *correctly* (*orthōs*) and *advantageously*
(*ōphelimōs*), do you then say that they are *controlling their
actions* (*sōphronein*), or the opposite?'

'They are controlling their actions,' he said.

'And do they not control their actions under the influence
of *self-control* (*sōphrosunē*)?'

'Necessarily,' he said.   b

'And is it the case that those who don't act correctly act
foolishly (*aphronōs*), and in so doing are not controlling
their actions?'

'Yes, I think so,' he said.

'So acting foolishly is the opposite of acting *in a self-
controlled manner* (*sōphronōs*)?'

He said it was.

'And is it the case that what is done foolishly is done
under the influence of *folly* (*aphrosunē*), and that what is
done in a self-controlled manner is done under the influence
of self-control?'

He agreed.

'And if something is done under the influence of strength
it is done strongly and if under the influence of weakness,
weakly?'

29

c   So he thought.

'And if with quickness, quickly, and if with slowness, slowly?'

It was.

'So whatever is done thus and so, is done under the influence of this and such a thing, and similarly for its opposite?'

He agreed.

'Now,' I said, 'is there such a thing as the *noble* (*kalon*)?'

'Yes.'

'And does it have any opposite but the *base* (*aischron*)?'

'No.'

'And such a thing as the *good*?'

'Yes.'

'Having any opposite but the *bad*?'

'No.'

'What about high pitch: is there such a thing?'

He said yes.

'Does it have any opposite but low?'

He said no.

'So,' I said, 'for each of the opposites there is one single opposite and no more?'

He continued to agree.

d   'Come now,' I said, 'let us reckon up what we have agreed so far. We are agreed that for each thing there is one single opposite and no more?'

'We are.'

'And that what is done in an opposite manner is done under the influence of an opposite?'

He said yes.

'And we are agreed that what is done *foolishly* (*aphronōs*) is done in an opposite manner from what is done *in a self-controlled manner* (*sōphronōs*)?'

He said yes.

'And that what is done *in a self-controlled manner* is done under the influence of *self-control* (*sōphrosunē*), while what is done foolishly is done under the influence of *folly* (*aphrosunē*)?'

He agreed.

e   'And since they are done in an opposite manner, they would each be done under the influence of an opposite?'

30

'Yes.'

'And one is done under the influence of *self-control* while the other is done under the influence of *folly*?'

'Yes.'

'In an opposite manner?'

'Absolutely.'

'Under the influence of opposites?'

'Yes.'

'So that folly is the opposite of self-control?'

'Apparently.'

'Well, do you recall our earlier agreement that folly is the opposite of *wisdom*?'

He did.

'And that to one thing there is one single opposite and no more?'

'I agree.'

'In that case, Protagoras, which of our two statements are   333a
we to give up: that one thing is the opposite of only one thing, or the claim that wisdom is a thing distinct from self-control, and that each is a part of excellence, and that in addition to being distinct they are also dissimilar both in themselves and in relation to their capacities, as with the parts of the face? Which are we to give up? The two state-ments are not in unison; they don't chime in well-tuned harmony together. How could they, when one thing can have only one opposite and no more, while wisdom and   b
self-control are each the opposite of folly, itself a single thing? That is how it is, isn't it, Protagoras; or would you have it otherwise?'

He agreed, though with great reluctance.

'Then wouldn't wisdom and self-control be one and the same thing? And what's more, we have already discovered that justice and holiness are more-or-less the same thing.'

Section XVI

'Come now, Protagoras,' I continued; 'let us not falter till we have completed our investigation. Would you ever say that a man who *commits an injustice (adikein) acts soundly (sōphronein)* in committing that injustice?'

c 'For my part, Socrates,' he said, 'I should be ashamed to make such an admission. But many people say so.'

'And shall I address myself to them,' I said, 'or to you?'

'If you like,' he said, 'address yourself first to the popular view.'

'It's all the same to me,' I said, 'whether the view is your own or not, just so long as you are giving the answers. For it is the view itself which I shall be testing; though it may turn out that it's both I who ask and you who answer who are being tested.'

d At first Protagoras tried to make excuses, and claimed that it was a complicated question. Finally, however, he agreed to answer.

'Come,' I said, 'let's go back to the beginning. Would you say that some men who *commit injustice (adikein) act soundly (sōphronein)*?'

'We shall assume so.'

'And when you say *act soundly*, you mean that they *exercise good sense (eu phronein)*?'

'Yes.'

'And when you say *good sense*, you mean that they *plan well (eubouleuesthai)* by committing those injustices?'

'Let us say that.'

'If they *do well (eu prattein)* in committing it, or if they do badly?'

'If they do well.'

'Do you call some things *good (agatha)*?'

'I do.'

'And what you call good,' I said, 'are things which are *beneficial (ōphelima)* to men?'

e 'Whether they are beneficial to men or not, by Zeus,' he said, 'I still call them good.'

It was obvious that Protagoras was riled and spoiling for a fight, setting out his answers in battle array. Realising this, I continued with more caution and asked gently: 'Are you referring to things which are beneficial to no man,
334a Protagoras, or to things which are not beneficial at all? Is that what you call good?'

Section XVI

'Not at all,' he said. 'I know plenty of things which are not beneficial to men – foods, drinks, drugs, thousands of things – and plenty which are beneficial. But there are many other things which are neither beneficial nor harmful to men but are beneficial to horses. Again there are some things which are beneficial only to cattle or to dogs; or to none of these, but to trees; or good for the roots of trees but bad for the shoots. Dung, for example, is good for all plants when applied to the roots, but utterly destructive when   b applied to the shoots and young branches. The same is true of olive oil, which is thoroughly bad for all plants and most inimical to the hair of all animals but man; in the case of man, however, it benefits the hair and the whole body. Indeed goodness is such a diverse and complex thing that even in this case the same thing can be good for a man when applied externally, but very bad when taken inter-   c nally. That is why doctors forbid sick patients to add more than the smallest quantity of oil to the food which they are to eat – just sufficient to overcome the unpleasantness that arises from food and savouries, and affects the senses through the nostrils.'

This point was greeted by general applause, as well made. And I said: 'Being, as it happens, a rather forgetful sort of person, Protagoras, I tend to forget, faced with a lengthy statement, the original point of the argument. Now, suppose   d I happened to be hard of hearing: if you meant to hold a conversation with me, you would think it necessary to speak more loudly than normal; so now that you are faced by a man with a poor memory, please cut your answers down and make them short enough for me to follow.'

'What do you mean, "make my answers short"? Am I to make them shorter than is necessary?' he said.

'Certainly not,' I said.

'As short as is necessary, then?' he said.

'Yes,' I said.   e

'Am I then to make my answers as short as I think necess- ary, or as short as you think necessary?'

'They do tell me,' I said, 'that you are adept both as an exponent and as a teacher of the art of speaking either at length, if you choose, so that you never run dry, or briefly,

335a so much so that no one could be more concise. So if you want to hold a discourse with me, please use the second technique – the brief one.'

'Socrates,' he said, 'I have debated against many men in my time; and if I had argued by the rules of debate laid down by my opponent, as you demand, I should have proved no better than the next man, and the name of Protagoras would not be celebrated throughout Greece.'

b Well I realised that he was dissatisfied with his performance so far, and would be reluctant to continue the discussion as answerer. So I decided that there was no longer any place for me in these proceedings, and said: 'Very well, Protagoras, I don't insist on holding a discussion on what you consider unsatisfactory terms. But I will only converse with you when you are prepared to talk in a way which I can follow. For you, so they say, are equally competent at

c conversing briefly or at length: after all, you are *wise*. I, on the other hand, am no good at these long speeches, however much I might wish it otherwise. But it was for you, who are good at both, to make a concession to me, and adopt the method suited to both of us, to make the conversation possible; as it is, since you aren't prepared to do so, and I have other business, and I am not able to wait while you spin out your long speeches – I have an urgent appointment, you see – so I am going. Otherwise I might not have been unwilling to listen even to your speeches.'

intervene

Section XVII

With these words I got up to leave. And as I was getting
d up Callias seized my hand with his right hand, this old coat of mine with his left, and said:

'We shan't let you go, Socrates; our discussion will not be the same if you leave. Do stay, I beg you. There is no one I should rather hear than Protagoras and you arguing it out. Please let us all have our way in this.'

And I said – on my feet by now, and ready to leave: 'Son

of Hipponicus, I have always admired your love of wisdom, and I certainly praise and love you for it now; so I should   e
willingly let you have your way if your request were a possible one to fulfill. But as it is you might as well beg me to keep up with Crison, the runner from Himera, in his peak form, or to match the speed of some long-distance or marathon runner. I should reply that, never mind you, I   336a
myself wish I could keep up with runners like these. But I can't. If for some reason it is necessary to watch me running in the same race as Crison, beg him to slow down: for I can't run fast, but he can run slowly. So if you desire to listen to Protagoras and me, beg him to answer briefly and to confine himself to the questions asked, as he did earlier. Otherwise,   b
what basis for discussion can there be between us? For my part, I used to think there was a difference between a companionable discussion and a public harangue!'

'But Socrates,' he said, 'you must see that Protagoras is quite justified in asking for the same right to argue his points in the manner he chooses as you yourself are.'

At this Alcibiades interrupted and said 'You're wrong, Callias. Socrates admits that he doesn't share Protagoras' aptitude for speaking at length, and defers to him; but when it comes to debate and skill in deploying and understanding   c
an argument I should be surprised if he came off second to any man. If, therefore, Protagoras in turn admits that he is inferior to Socrates in debate, Socrates is content. If, on the other hand, he pretends otherwise, let him discuss the issue by means of question and answer instead of spinning out long speeches in response to every question, and avoiding the argument by refusing to give a reasoned account of his   d
own position, and instead going on and on until most of his audience have forgotten the point of the question in the first place – except Socrates, that is: I have a suspicion he won't forget, in spite of his little joke about having a poor memory. So in my opinion Socrates' position is the fairer – after all, everyone must express his own point of view.'

After Alcibiades, the next to speak, as I recall, was Critias, who turned to Prodicus and Hippias and said:

'In my opinion, Callias is highly biased towards Protagoras, while Alcibiades is always concerned to get his way   e

35

in any enterprise. But we shouldn't take sides with Socrates or Protagoras in their jealous rivalry but beg them both equally not to break up our meeting.'

337a   At these words Prodicus said: 'I quite agree, Critias. Those who are present at such discussions ought to give a hearing to both sides equally but not give both sides an equal hearing. There is a distinction: one must hear both sides equally yet not give equal weight to both, but more to the wiser and less to the more ignorant. My opinion, Protagoras and Socrates, is that you should agree to argue the topic and not

b   to debate it: for whereas argument is conducted amicably among friends, debate takes place between antagonists and adversaries. The former will be the most proper atmosphere for our discourse. For you, by speaking in this spirit, will win our respect, not praise (respect being the sincerely felt disposition of us, your audience, as opposed to praise, which

c   is a frequently insincere verbal expression of regard); while we, by listening, shall experience delight, not pleasure (delight being an intellectual feeling experienced by one engaged in the activity of thought and learning, as opposed to pleasure, which is an agreeable sensation accompanying such purely physical activities as eating).'

When Prodicus had finished, a large number of the company agreed with him. But after him the wise Hippias spoke:

'Gentlemen,' he said, 'I believe that all of us here are brothers, friends and compatriots, not by *convention* (*nomos*)

d   but by *nature* (*phusis*). For by nature it is affinity which makes us brothers, whereas convention, that tyrant of humanity, often violates nature by compulsion. What ignominy it is, then, that we should know the nature of things and yet, when we assemble together, we the *leading experts* (*sophōtatoi*) of Hellas, in this sacred hearth of Hellenic *knowledge* (*sophia*), and in that very city's greatest and most magnificent household, in pursuit of that very knowledge – that we should have nothing to show worthy of this

e   noble renown but fall to bickering among ourselves like the most vulgar of mankind. I therefore urge and implore you, Protagoras and Socrates, to be reconciled through our me-

338a   diating arbitration. Socrates, do not insist on this rigorous

and excessively brief form of discourse, if it displeases Protagoras, but ease off and hold a looser rein on your discussions and so make them grander and more elegant; Protagoras, do not spread all sail to the wind and take refuge on an ocean of words, concealing dry land from view. Take a middle course, both of you. Do as I suggest and choose someone to be umpire, chairman and president who can ensure a moderate length of argument on the part of   b each of you.'

The gathering approved of this proposal and everyone praised Hippias. Moreover Callias insisted that he would not let me go, while everyone begged me to select a chairman. So I pointed out that it would be invidious to appoint a referee over the arguments, 'since,' I said, 'the man you appoint will either be inferior to us, in which case he will be in no position to judge between the better and the worse, or he will be our equal, in which case he will still be in no position to judge: for our equal will do the same as we do, so that his appointment will be otiose. "Ah," you may say,   c "but we shall appoint a man who is your superior." But in my opinion it is in fact impossible to choose anyone wiser than Protagoras, whereas if you select a man who is no better and claim that he is, this too will be a personal affront to Protagoras, as though you were appointing someone to preside over a nobody, though for myself I shouldn't mind at all. But I should like to adopt the following procedure to enable us to conduct the meeting and discussion which you desire. If Protagoras doesn't wish to be the answerer, then   d let him ask the questions while I give the answers; and at the same time I shall try to give him an illustration of what I consider to be the correct way to reply to questions. Then, when I have answered as many questions as he chooses to ask, let him likewise in his turn submit to my cross-questioning. In that case, if it turns out that he is reluctant to answer the actual question asked, I can join with you in begging him not to break up our gathering, just as you did with me a moment ago. Moreover this procedure needs no   e single presiding officer, since you will all be presiding together.'

This proposal was accepted, and although Protagoras was

37

very reluctant, he was forced to agree first to be the questioner and then when he had asked enough questions, to take his turn at giving only brief replies.

Section XVIII

Protagoras began his questioning something like this:

'I believe, Socrates,' he said, 'personally, that the greatest mark of education in a man is his skill at discussing verses; that is to say, his ability to discriminate what is sound from what is unsound in a poet's writings, and to give a reasoned account in reply to questions. Indeed my question still concerns the topic which you and I were discussing just now – excellence, that is – but transferred to the context of poetry; that will be the only difference. Simonides, in a poem addressed to Scopas the son of Creon of Thessaly, says:

339a

b
To *be* (*genesthai*)* a good man in truth, *I admit* (*men*),†
is *hard* (*chalepon*) – a man in mind and frame
a flawless minting foursquare struck.

Do you know the lyric, or shall I recite the whole thing for you?'

And I said: 'There's no need. Not only do I know the song, it so happens that I have made a detailed study of it.'

'Good,' he said. 'Then do you find it well and soundly composed, or not?'

'Most excellently and soundly,' I said.

'But do you think that a poem in which the poet contradicts himself is well composed?'

'No,' I said.

---

* Both *genesthai* and *emmenai* (or *einai*) can properly be translated 'to be.' But *genesthai* is the past infinitive of the verb *gignesthai*, which means 'to become'; hence colloquially *genesthai* can mean either to become or to be (i.e. to have become). The argument which follows depends on this ambiguity.

† Technically *men* is a particle (meaning 'on the one hand') which is used to prepare the reader for a later idea (introduced by *de*: 'on the other hand') which is contrasted with or actually opposed to the first idea.

Section XVIII

'Then look,' he said, 'more closely.'

'But my dear fellow,' I said, 'I have looked quite closely c enough.'

'Then you will be aware,' he said, 'that a little later in the poem he says:

> Yet (de) Pittacus' familiar words, I find, do not
> ring true, though they come from a wise man;
> It is *hard* (*chalepon*), he said, to *be* (*emmenai*) noble.

You realise that it is the same man who both says this and wrote the previous lines?'

'I know,' I said.

'Then do you think,' he said, 'that the second statement is consistent with the first?'

'So it seems to me,' I said, although I feared he might have a point. 'Why, doesn't it seem so to you?'

'How can the man who makes both these statements d appear to be consistent, when he begins with the premise that it is hard to be a good man in truth, and then a little further on in the poem forgets, and criticises Pittacus, who says the same as he does, that it is hard to be noble, and refuses to accept his statement which is identical with his own? Yet when he criticises the man who says the same as he does, he evidently criticises himself, so that either his first or his second statement is not sound.'

These words produced general applause and praise among the audience. And at first, like a man struck by a skilful e boxer, my eyes went dim and my head reeled at his words and at the applause of the others. Then – and to be perfectly candid with you, I was trying to gain time to think out what the poet did mean – I turned and called on Prodicus.

'Prodicus,' I said, 'Simonides is a fellow-citizen of yours; so you are the right person to come to the man's assistance. 340a So I think I shall call upon you. As the river Scamander called upon the Simoeis, in Homer, when it was beset by Achilles, with the words "Dear brother, let us together check his mighty onslaught," so I call upon you: let not Protagoras reduce Simonides to ruins. For now, you see, Simonides' rescue requires the art of which you gave such a fine demonstration just now: that of drawing distinctions b

39

between such things as "wishing" and "desiring". See if you agree with me on this point. Simonides does not seem to be contradicting himself. But first, Prodicus, give me your opinion: do you think *genesthai* is the same as *einai*, or different?'   *being*   *becoming*

'Oh surely different,' said Prodicus.

'And at the beginning Simonides gave his own opinion when he said that to *be* (*genesthai*) a good man was in truth hard?'

c   'That's right,' said Prodicus

become good
be good

'And when he criticises Pittacus,' I said, 'he does not, as Protagoras supposes, thereby criticise the same statement as he himself had made, but a different one. For Pittacus' statement was not that it is hard to *be* (*genesthai*) good, as Simonides stated, but that it is hard to *be* (*emmenai*) good. But as Prodicus here says, Protagoras, *genesthai* and *einai* aren't the same thing. And if *einai* and *genesthai* aren't the same, it follows that Simonides doesn't contradict himself. Indeed, perhaps Prodicus and many others besides would

d   agree that it is hard to *be* (*genesthai*) good. As Hesiod says: "The gods have placed sweat on the path to virtue; but when virtue's summit is mounted it is thenceforth an easy attainment, though it was hard to gain." '

Prodicus approved my words; but Protagoras said: 'The rescue is worse than the error from which you seek to rescue him, Socrates.'

'Then I have done harm, Protagoras,' I replied, 'and I am,

e   it seems, an absurd physician, whose treatment has aggravated the disease.'

'I'm afraid that's so,' he said.

'Why?' I asked.

'The poet must be exceedingly foolish,' he replied, 'if he thinks that excellence is so trivial a thing as to be regarded as an easy attainment when it is the hardest of all, as everyone agrees.'

And I said: 'By Zeus, what a happy coincidence that Prodicus should be here for our discussion. You see, Protagoras,

341a   I suspect that Prodicus' *knowledge* (*sophia*) is both divine and ancient – going back to Simonides or perhaps even further. Yet it would seem that you yourself, learned as you

40

are in many other fields, are not familiar with this one – not as familiar as I who have studied under Prodicus here. For in the present case I don't think you appreciate that Simonides didn't understand by *"hard"* (*chalepon*) in this context what you understand. Take the word *"terrible"* (*deinos*); each time I use the word to praise someone like yourself and say that "Protagoras is a terribly wise man", Prodicus corrects me and asks if I'm not ashamed to call bad what is good. For what is terrible, he says, is bad. At any rate no one speaks ever of "terrible wealth" or "terrible peace" or "terrible healthiness", but of "terrible illness" and "terrible war" and "terrible poverty", since what is terrible is bad. Thus perhaps by "hard" Simonides and other Ceians understand "bad" or something like that, without your realising it. Let's ask Prodicus – for it's fair to ask him about Simonides' dialect. What did Simonides mean by "hard", Prodicus?'

' "Bad",' he said.

'And so presumably, Prodicus,' I said, 'that's why he criticised Pittacus for saying "It's hard to be noble", as though he understood him to mean that it's bad to be noble.'

'Why, what else do you think Simonides means, Socrates,' he said. 'He's attacking Pittacus for the fact that being from Lesbos and educated in a barbarous dialect he was incapable of properly distinguishing the meanings of words.'

'You hear Prodicus,' I said to Protagoras. 'What do you have to say to that?'

'That's quite wrong, Prodicus,' he said. 'I know perfectly well that Simonides meant by "hard" precisely what everyone else means: not "bad" but "that which is not easy and is accomplished only with great effort".'

'In my opinion, Protagoras,' I said, 'not only is that what Simonides meant, but Prodicus knows it was, and is joking and wants to see if you are capable of rescuing your own argument. For there is strong evidence that Simonides didn't mean "bad" by "hard" in the passage which immediately follows, where he says "A god alone could have that privilege." He would hardly say that it's bad to be noble, and go on to say that nobility belongs to the god alone, and so confine this privilege to the god alone: if so, Prodicus

b

c

d

e

41

342a would be accusing Simonides, a fellow Ceian, of villainy. But if you really want to make the discussion of verses the test, as you claim, of my ability, I should like to explain what I think Simonides means in his lyric; or if you wish I shall listen to you.'

Now Protagoras, hearing me say this, said, 'If you want, Socrates.' But Prodicus and Hippias and the others warmly urged me to go ahead.

Section XIX

'Well now,' I said, 'I shall try to expound my interpretation of the lyric. In all Greece, philosophy has the strongest and most long-established tradition in Crete and Lacedae-
b mon [Sparta]; and it is there that the largest number of sophists is to be found. But, like the men whom Protagoras was calling sophists, they deny this and pretend to be uneducated, in order to prevent people from finding out that their dominance in Greece is due to their *wisdom*, and they prefer to give the impression that it is due to their military superiority and courage. For they think that if people found out the secret of their power then everyone would cultivate wisdom. And their deceit has quite fooled laconizers [pro-Spartans] in the Greek cities who, in their attempts to copy
c them, sport cauliflower ears and don boxing gloves, indulge in physical training and wear short cloaks, under the impression that such things have made Sparta a power among the Greeks. Now when the Spartans are tired of discoursing with their sophists in secret and wish to do so openly, they put an expulsion order on all foreigners in the country, including the laconizers among them, and consort with their sophists without the knowledge of any foreigner.
d Moreover, like the Cretans, they forbid their young to travel abroad in case they should unlearn all that they themselves have taught them at home. Indeed, in Sparta and Crete it is not only men who take pride in their education, but women as well.

42

Section XIX

'And here is how you can tell that I am right and that the Spartans are the best-trained in philosophy and argument. Anyone who talks even to the dullest Spartan will find that while for most of the time he seems rather dull in his speech, at some point in the conversation he will throw out a striking aphorism, short and pithy, like a crack shot, and make his companion look like a mere child. And some people, both now and in the past, have realised that laconizing was a matter of the pursuit not of good physique but of wisdom, knowing that the ability to make this kind of saying is the mark of a truly educated man. Among these are numbered Thales of Miletus, Pittacus of Mytilene, Bias of Priene, our own Solon, Cleobulus of Lindos, Myson of Chen, and, seventh, the Spartan Chilon. All these men admired, emulated and studied the Spartan form of education. If you want proof that their wisdom consisted of short memorable sayings, remember that they went to Delphi together and, on the temple there, dedicated to Apollo the first fruits of their wisdom in the sayings "Know thyself" and "Nothing in excess".

'Why am I telling you all this? Because this literally laconic terseness was the traditional style of philosophy. And this saying of Pittacus, "It's hard to be noble", was privately circulated among the wise men and highly praised by them. Now Simonides, anxious for a reputation for wisdom, realised that if he attacked this saying and defeated it, then, just as if he had defeated a famous athlete, he would become famous in his own time. So I think he wrote the entire poem as an attack on this saying of Pittacus in order to discredit it.

'Let's study it together and see if I am right. And straight away the opening of the poem would obviously be mad if he meant to say that it is hard to *be* (*genesthai*) good but qualified it with "*I admit* (*men*)".* This qualification seems complete nonsense unless you take it to be directed at Pittacus' words, and assume that Simonides is speaking contentiously, saying, as it were, in reply to Pittacus' claim that "it's hard to *be* (*emmenai*) noble", "No it isn't Pittacus;

*See above, p. 38n.

343a

b

c

d

e

43

it's *becoming* (*genesthai*) good that's truly hard" – not, notice, truly good: it isn't that word to which the word "truth"
belongs, as though he meant that among all good things
some were truly good while others were good but not truly
so; that would be too naïve for Simonides. Rather we must
understand the position of the words "in truth" as a hyper-
baton; thus we may imagine Pittacus' words coming first,
as if he were speaking them himself, and then Simonides
replying. First Pittacus: "O mortals, it is hard to *be* (*emmenai*) noble." Then Simonides: "O Pittacus, that isn't true.
Not to *be* (*einai*) good, but to *become* (*genesthai*) good, in
mind and frame a flawless minting foursquare struck – *that*
is the hard thing in truth." Thus, it becomes clear that the
insertion of "*I admit* (*men*)" makes sense and the words "in
truth" find their correct position at the end. Moreover what
follows proves that this is his meaning. Indeed I could provide abundant proofs of the poem's excellent composition at
each point; it is both carefully constructed and full of charm.
Since, however, it would take too long to go through the
entire poem in that way, let us examine its general character and meaning to see how above all it is in its entirety
a rebuttal of Pittacus' saying. A little further on he says, if
we imagine him developing an argument, that whereas it
is truly hard to become a good man but possible for a short
while, "yet according to you, Pittacus, having once reached
that state, to remain in it and *be* (*einai*) a good man is
impossible and superhuman since 'A god alone could have
that privilege',

. . . while a man
can not escape *being* (*emmenai*) bad
dragged down by helpless circumstance.

Now who is dragged down by helpless circumstance in the
command of a ship? Not the private passenger evidently,
since he already was down in the first place: you cannot
cast down someone who is already on the ground; it is the
man who is on his feet that can be cast down and put on
the ground, not the man who already is on the ground. In
the same way it is only the resourceful who can be dragged
down by helpless circumstance, not the man who already is

helpless. So too the onset of a great storm might render a steersman helpless, or the advent of a bad season might leave a farmer helpless, or similarly in the case of a doctor. For it is possible for the noble to become bad, as is shown by these words from another poet:

But a good man is bad sometimes
as well as noble at others.

But for the bad man, not only is it impossible for him to   e
become bad; of necessity he already is continuously bad. Thus when helpless circumstance drags down the resourceful, wise and excellent man, he cannot escape being bad. But you claim, Pittacus, that it is hard to be noble, whereas in fact *becoming* noble is hard (but possible), but to *be* noble is impossible:

For if he does well, any man is good,
but bad if he does badly.

Now of what does doing well at letters consist, and what   345a
makes a man do well at letters? Clearly, the knowledge of letters. Or in what respect does a man do well to be a good doctor? Clearly the knowledge of healing the sick. 'But bad if he does badly': now who could become a bad doctor? Clearly the man who has the property first of being a doctor, then, in addition, of being a good doctor. For such a man can in turn become bad, whereas we laymen could never by doing badly become doctors, builders or anything of the sort; and a man who cannot become a doctor by doing badly   b clearly cannot become a bad doctor either. Thus, while the good man might become bad as a result of time or overwork or illness or some similar misfortune (for this is the only respect in which a man can do badly – by deprivation of knowledge) the bad man could never become bad, because he already was bad in the first place; if, then, he is to become bad, he will first have to become good. So this part of the poem is to the same purpose, that while to be a good man (in the sense of persistently good) is not possible, becoming   c good is possible, and similarly for badness: 'While best for longest are those whom the gods love.' "

'And it is not only these remarks which are directed at

Pittacus. The following passages in the lyric would make the point even more clearly. He says:

So I'll not waste my lifetime's meagre ration
on an empty dream, in search of what can never
ever *be* (*genesthai*): that flawless man
among us who for our living
toil in the broad earth;
d   Should I find one I'll let you know.

Thus throughout the poem he inveighs against Pittacus' saying:

I praise and love all men
who do no *evil* (*aischron*) willingly (*hekōn*);
even the gods
do not combat necessity.

This too makes the same point. For Simonides was not so untutored as to declare his praise of everyone who *willingly* does no *evil* (*kakon*), as though there were people who willingly do evil. For I suspect no wise man thinks that any
e   man willingly goes astray or willingly acts badly and disgracefully. They know perfectly well that all who do what is *shameful* (*aischron*) and *bad* (*kakon*) do so against their will. So in Simonides' case, he is not saying he praises anyone who does not do evil willingly, but is rather applying the word "willingly" to himself. For he considered that a *noble man* (*kalos k'agathos*) frequently finds himself in the
346a   position of having to force himself to love and praise someone – say, an estranged mother or father, or country, or whatever it may be. So when bad men found themselves in this position, he believed, they observed with glee the wickedness of their parents or mother country and critically pointed out and condemned it, in the hope of avoiding opprobrium for neglecting them, so that they even redoubled
b   their rebukes, and willingly added enmities to those they couldn't avoid; the good, on the other hand, are forced to cover up and praise them, and should they be indignant at some wrong inflicted by their parents or their state, they calm and soothe their own anger and compel themselves to love and praise their own kin. Now Simonides too, I think, frequently felt that he was eulogising a tyrant or someone

46

Section XIX

of that kind, not willingly but under compulsion. Thus in   c
Pittacus' case, he tells him: "Pittacus, my reason for blaming you is not that I'm harsh judge, since 'good enough for me the man who's not all bad,'

> nor lawless to excess,
> who knows the worth of justice, bastion of cities;
> a sound man: I'll find no fault with him.

For I'm not a fault-finding kind of man.

Without number the breed of fools.

So if anyone does take delight in criticising, let him find fault, to his heart's content, with them.

You see, all things are *noble* (*kala*)
which bear not *evil's* (*aischra*) taint."

Now he says this not as one might say "All things are white   d
which bear no taint of black". That would be silly in many ways. Rather, he means that he tolerates without censure the middle course. "I am not seeking," he is saying,

> "that flawless man
> among us who for our living
> toil in the broad earth;
> Should I find one I'll let you know.

Therefore I shan't actually praise anyone. Good enough for me the man who finds the middle way and does nothing bad because:

I praise and love all men. . ."

. . . here, by the way, he has employed the Mytilenean dialect as though it were for Pittacus' benefit that he said "I   e
praise and love all men willingly" – it is here with this clause that we must take the word "willingly" – with "I praise and love" – "though there are some whom I praise and love against my will. As for you, Pittacus, if your words had even been moderately reasonable and true, I should   347a
never have criticised you. But as it is, you have the reputation of being right on a most serious matter though what you say is profoundly wrong; and because of that I do criticise you."

47

The Protagoras

'That, Prodicus and Protagoras, is what, in my view, Simonides meant in this poem.'

Here Hippias spoke up. 'A good account of the poem,
b Socrates,' he said. 'And I,' he added, 'also have a rather good
interpretation of it myself which I will expound, if you like.'

'Yes, Hippias,' said Alcibiades, 'some other time, perhaps.
But right now it is time for Protagoras' and Socrates' agreement to be fulfilled; Protagoras must either ask questions
for Socrates to answer or, if he wants to answer Socrates'
questions he must let Socrates do the questioning.'

'I leave Protagoras to choose whichever course he finds
the more agreeable,' I said. 'With his permission let us give
c up songs and poetry, but I should be delighted to complete
our mutual examination of the questions I raised with you,
Protagoras, a while ago. Intellectual discourse on poetry, it
seems to me, is very like the drinking parties of common
unsophisticated types who, because of their inability to provide their own voices or their own conversation while they
d drink – such is their lack of education – bid up the price of
flute-girls, and pay large fees to hire the extraneous voice
of the flute and so accompany their evening with its voice
to compensate for their own lack of conversation. But when
the companions are *well-bred (kaloi k'agathoi)* and educated
you won't find flute-girls, dancing girls or female acrobats:
they are capable of entertaining themselves by the use of
their own voices, without silly fun and games of that sort,
taking their turns at speaking and listening in good order
e even after they have drunk deeply. So it should be in the
case of gatherings like this, with men of the sort most of us
claim to be; there is no need for an extraneous voice or for
poets, who cannot be asked to explain their meaning, while
the vulgar introduce them into their conversations and offer
varying explanations of a poet's meaning, since they are
discussing a subject in which they aren't open to refutation.
No, they leave such debates alone and provide each other
348a with their own entertainment through the medium of their
own discourse, testing and being tested by each other. Such
are the people you and I should emulate, in my view: we
should set aside the poets and hold discourse directly with
one another, putting ourselves to the test of truth. And I

48

Section XX

am willing to continue to submit to your questions if that
is what you prefer; or, if you like, you can submit to my
questions, in a thorough and complete investigation of the
matters we broke off just now.'

Section XX

These, and more to the same effect, were my words; and   b
when Protagoras would give no clear sign of what he meant
to do, Alcibiades turned to Callias and said:

'Do you approve of Protagoras' conduct in refusing to
make it clear whether he will take up the argument or not?
I certainly don't. Let him either take up the discussion or
say that he doesn't want to do so; then we shall all know,
and Socrates can debate with someone else, or else two
others can take up the argument.'

Protagoras seemed to me to be stung by this, because at   c
these words of Alcibiades, and with Callias and most of the
others adding their pleas, he reluctantly agreed to take up
the discussion and told me that I could ask the questions
while he answered.

So I said: 'Protagoras, you musn't think I'm arguing with
you for any other purpose than the investigation of questions by which I myself am constantly puzzled. Homer made
an important point, in my view, when he said:

When two go in company, one sees before the other.   d

I suppose that in this way we are all more inventive in
every enterprise, discussion and conception; but "if one sees
by himself" then he immediately goes round looking for a
man with whom he can share his discovery and confirm it,
until he finds someone. Which is why I should rather hold
a discussion with you than with any other man. For I think
you are the best man to examine important matters suitable
for rational inquiry, and particularly *excellence*. After all,   e
who better? Not only do you consider yourself a *noble and
excellent man* (*kalos k'agathos*), a quality which you share
with others who, although they are decent men themselves,

49

349a nevertheless cannot also make other men good, but you are both good yourself and are able to make other men good. And such is your confidence in yourself that where others conceal this skill, you publicly advertise yourself to the whole of Greece, call yourself a sophist, declare yourself a teacher of education and excellence, and were the first to charge a fee for this. Mustn't I therefore invite you to investigate these matters, and ask questions and consult with you? Of course I must.

'But now, to return to the subject of my earlier questions, I should like you to go back to the beginning and refresh my memory about some points, and to join with me in the

b investigation of others. My question, as I recall, was this: *wisdom, moderation, courage (andreia), justice* and *holiness* are five names; but do they name the same thing, or does some distinct essence or thing uniquely correspond with each of them, such that each has its own unique capacity, and that no one of them is the same kind of thing as any other? To this you replied that they are not names for a

c single thing, but that each of these names uniquely denotes a distinct thing, and that all these are parts of excellence; not, however, as the parts of gold which are like each other and the whole of which they are parts, but as the parts of a face, both unlike the whole of which they are parts and unlike each other, each having its own unique capacity. If you are of the same opinion as before, say so; if of a different opinion, explain it precisely. I'm not holding you to any view, if you now say something else; for I shouldn't be

d surprised if you were just trying me out when you said that.'

'My reply to you, Socrates,' he said, 'is that these are indeed all parts of excellence, and that while four of them are tolerably close to each other, *courage* is absolutely different from all of them. You can see the truth of my words in this way: you will find many men who are utterly *unjust (adikos), unholy (anhosios)*, unruly and *ignorant (amathēs)* who are nevertheless exceedingly *courageous (andreios)*.'

e 'Come,' I said, 'your point deserves investigation. Do you call the courageous *daring (tharraleoi)*, or something else?'

'Oh, daring,' he said; 'and they readily go to meet what many fear to face.'

50

Section XX

'Well now,' I said, 'do you agree that excellence is something *admirable (kalon)* and that you offer yourself as a teacher of it, assuming it to be something admirable?'

'Oh, the most admirable,' he said, 'unless I'm mad.'

'Then is part of it *base (aischron)*,' I said, 'and part of it admirable, or is it all admirable?'

'Oh, obviously all admirable – as admirable as can be.'

'Then you know that some men dive into wells *daringly (tharraleōs)*?'   350a

'Yes, I do: divers.'

'Because of their *knowledge (epistēmē)*, or for some other reason?'

'Because of their knowledge.'

'And who are daring at fighting on horseback? Is it the ones who have horsemanship or the ones without horsemanship?'

'The ones who have horsemanship.'

'And what about fighting with light shields? Is it the experienced light infantrymen or not?'

'The experienced light infantrymen. And in general, if that's what you want to know,' he said, 'those who have knowledge are more daring than those who don't, while they themselves are more daring after acquiring it than they were before they acquired it.'

'And,' said I, 'have you never come across people with no   b
knowledge of any of these things, who are nevertheless daring at all of them?'

'Oh yes,' he said, 'only too daring.'

'And are these daring men also courageous?'

'Well, in that case,' he said, 'courage would be a *despicable thing (aischron)*: such men are crazy.'

'So what do you mean by the *courageous*?' I said. 'Didn't you say they were the *daring*?'

'I still do,' he said.

'And isn't it clear,' I said, 'that men who are daring in   c
this way are not courageous but crazy? And again that the *wisest (sophōtatoi)* are the most daring? And being the most daring, the most courageous? And that, according to this argument, *wisdom* would be *courage*?'

'You haven't correctly recalled what I was saying in an-

51

swer to your questions, Socrates,' he said. 'When you asked if the courageous were daring, I agreed; but you did not ask if the daring were courageous. If you had asked me at the

d   time, I should have said not always: but you have nowhere proved that when I agreed that the courageous were daring, my statement was wrong. What you in fact proved was that those with knowledge are more daring both than they themselves would otherwise have been, and then others who lack knowledge, and you therefore think courage and wisdom are the same thing. This would, by analogy, lead you to suppose that *strength* (*ischus*) is wisdom. For if, going on, you began by asking me if the *strong* (*ischuroi*) are *powerful*

e   (*dunatoi*), I should say yes. Next you would ask if those who have knowledge of wrestling have greater physical power than those with none, and are more powerful after learning to wrestle than before, and I should agree. Armed with these admissions you would then be in a position to say, advancing exactly the same proofs, that on my own admission strength is wisdom. But nowhere do I concede even in this last instance that the physically powerful are the strong, but only that the strong are physically powerful. For

351a   physical power and strength aren't the same, since power can be the result equally of knowledge or madness and rage, whereas strength comes from *nature* (*phusis*) and *proper physical training* (*eutrophia tōn somatōn*). Similarly in our case I can say that daring and courage aren't the same thing; so it follows that the courageous are daring but the daring aren't always courageous. For men acquire their

b   daring both from skill and from anger or madness, like their physical power, but courage comes from nature and the *proper training of the mind* (*eutrophia tēs psuchēs*).'

Section XXI

'And you agree, Protagoras,' I said, 'that some men *live well* (*eu zēn*) and others *badly* (*kakōs*)?'
He did.

Section XXI

'Well, do you think a man would be living well if he lived in pain and misery?'

He didn't.

'What about the man who lived out his life *pleasantly* (*hēdeōs*)? I suppose you think that, in that case, he would have lived well?'

'It seems so to me,' he said.

'Then living *pleasantly* (*hēdeōs*) is good and living unpleasantly is bad?'

'If, that is, the things one *enjoyed* (*hēdesthai*) in life were   c
worthy of respect (*kala*)' he said.

'What's this, Protagoras? Surely you don't agree with *ordinary people* (*hoi polloi*) that some *pleasant things* (*hēdea*) are *bad* (*kaka*) and some *painful things* (*aniara*) are *good* (*agatha*); I mean, insofar as things are *pleasant* (*hēdea*) are they not, *qua* pleasant, good, disregarding any possible consequences? And similarly with painful things: are they not, *qua* painful, bad?'

'Socrates,' he said, 'I'm not sure I ought to give the un-   d
qualified response your question invites and say that the desirable (*hēdu*) is always good and the painful always bad. Rather, bearing in mind not only your present question but also my life as a whole, I think it would be safest to reply that some things which are *desirable* aren't good, that some painful things aren't bad while others are good, and that there is a third group which is neither good nor bad.'

'You mean by "*desirable*",' I said, 'involving or producing *pleasure* (*hēdonē*)?'

'Quite,' he said.   e

'I mean this,' I said. 'Insofar as they are *desirable* are they not *good* – in other words, isn't *pleasure* itself good?'

'As you keep saying,' he said, 'let us examine the question, and if our thesis seems reasonable and the pleasant turns out to be the same as the good, we shall agree; if not, then will be the time to disagree.'

'In that case,' I said, 'do you wish to lead the inquiry, or am I to take the lead?'

'You are the proper one to take the lead,' he said; 'after all, you raised the question.'

'Well,' I said, 'perhaps it would become clear in this way.   352a

53

The Protagoras

Suppose a man were examining someone for health or some similar bodily function; he might look at the face and hands and then say: "Now undress and show me your chest and back as well, so that I can examine you more thoroughly." I desire to do something like that in the case of our inquiry. Now that I have examined you for your disposition in relation in relation to the *pleasant* (*hēdu*) and the *good* (*agathon*), and have found it to be as you say it is, I want to say something like this: "Come now, Protagoras, show me your
b   attitude to this: what is your disposition in relation to *knowledge* (*epistēmē*)? Do you agree with the general opinion, or do you disagree? For the general opinion about knowledge is more or less as follows: it isn't a strong or guiding or controlling element. And not only do people have this opinion about knowledge, but they also believe that in many cases where knowledge is present in a man, it is not the knowledge that controls him, but something else – now anger, now pleasure, now pain, now love, often fear – think-
c   ing of knowledge just as one does of a slave, as something dragged along behind all the other elements. Now is this the sort of view you have of it, or do you think knowledge is admirable and capable of controlling a man, such that if a man knew what is good and bad, nothing could overpower this knowledge or force the man to do anything other than what it dictates, since his intelligence provides the man with sufficient support?" '
d   'I agree with what you say,' he said. 'Indeed, it would be *shameful* (*aischron*) if I of all people didn't agree that wisdom or knowledge is the most powerful of all human qualities.'

'An admirable and correct reply,' I said. 'You know that most people don't agree with us; they say that there are many who know what is best and are in a position to do it, but nevertheless refuse to do so and do otherwise. And whenever I ask people how on earth they account for this, they say they behave in this way because they're overcome
e   by pleasure, or pain, or one of the things I mentioned.'

'Yes, Socrates,' he said, 'but people are mistaken about many other subjects too.'

'Very well, join me in the attempt to persuade and teach

54

people the nature of this experience of being overcome by   353a
pleasure and consequently of not doing what is best
although they know it to be what is best. For when we say
to them "What you say is not true; you are wrong," they
might ask us: "Protagoras and Socrates, if this experience
isn't that of being overcome by desire, what, pray, is it?
What do you say it is?" '

'But Socrates, why do we have to examine the opinion of
the mass of mankind who say the first thing that comes into
their head?'

'I think,' I said, 'that it will help us in our inquiry into   b
courage and the relation between it and the other parts of
excellence. So if you wish to abide by your previous agreement that I should lead the way on whatever path I think
most likely to lead us to the truth about courage, which I
think would be the best way of discovering the answer, then
you follow. Or if you don't wish to . . . if it suits you, I'll
drop the whole question.'

'You're right,' he said. 'Continue as you began.'

Section XXII

'Suppose,' I said, 'they went on to ask: "What, then,   c
according to you, is this phenomenon which we call being
overcome by *desire* (*hēdonē*)?" My own answer would be:
"Listen, while Protagoras and I try to tell you. Do you agree
that the phenomenon you describe is quite simply the common experience of doing what we know to be bad, overcome
by pleasures like food, drink or sex?" They would agree.
You and I should then continue with our questions: "In
what respect do you say such things are undesirable? Is it   d
because each of them causes immediate short-term *pleasure*
(*hēdonē*) and is *pleasant* (*hēdu*) only in the short term, or
because they store up illness, poverty and such like for the
future? Or would they still be bad even if they held no
trouble in store and produced nothing but pleasure, no matter how or why?" Do we expect, Protagoras, that they would

give any other answer than that they are bad, not in virtue of their immediate propensity to induce pleasure, but rather
e because of the ensuing illnesses and so on?'

'For myself,' said Protagoras, 'I think this would be most people's answer.'

'And asked if such things cause suffering by causing ill-
354a ness and poverty, they would agree, I imagine?'

Protagoras assented.

' "So you can see," we should continue, "that just as Protagoras and I were saying, they are bad merely because they result either in suffering or deprivation of other pleasure." Would they agree?'

We both thought they would agree.

'Why don't we proceed to ask them the converse: "You men who also claim that some unpleasant things are good – aren't you thinking of things like physical training and military service, and medical treatments which involve cautery, surgery, drugs and starvation diets, and of the fact that they are good but unpleasant?" They would say yes?'

He agreed.

b ' "Very well, and is your reason for calling them good the fact that their immediate result is extreme pain and suffering, or isn't it the fact that at a later time they result in cures, and physical health, and the safety of the city, and power over others, and wealth?" They would say yes, I think.'

He agreed.

' "Then are these things good for any other reason than because they lead in the end to pleasure and release from,
c or prevention of, pain? Or is there any end result other than pleasure and pain to explain why you call things good?" They would say they couldn't, I think.'

'I don't think they could either,' agreed Protagoras.

' "Therefore you seek pleasure as being good, while you avoid pain as being bad?" '

He agreed.

' "In that case by bad you must mean painful, and by good, pleasant, since you say that even enjoyment is bad when it either deprives people of greater pleasure than it produces or causes pain greater than the pleasure it pro-

vides; after all, if you had some other aspect or consequence   d
of pleasure in mind when you called it bad, you could tell
us what it was: but you can't." '

'No indeed they can't,' agreed Protagoras.

' "And conversely the same argument applies to suffering
pain, I suppose. You call pain good either when it frees
people from greater pain than it induces, or when it causes
greater pleasure than pain? For if, when you call suffering
good, you have some consequence in mind other than the   e
one I have just mentioned, you can tell us what it is. But
you won't be able to do so." '

'You're right,' said Protagoras.

' "To continue," ' I said, ' "if you were to ask me 'What on
earth has all this rigmarole got to do with the question?' I
should reply: 'Pardon me, in the first place it isn't easy to
explain what exactly it is that you mean by being overcome
by pleasure, and secondly my entire argument hinges on
this point.' But even now you may make a different move
if you have some way of maintaining that the good is some-   355a
thing other than pleasure, or that the bad is something
other than pain – or are you satisfied to live out your life
pleasantly and free from pain? If, on the other hand, you
are satisfied and have no other account of good and bad to
offer which does not amount in the end to this one, I shall
tell you what follows. I declare that in view of this fact,
your statement has become absurd: I mean when you say
that often a man, knowing the bad for what it is, still does
it, led on and thrown into confusion by pleasure; and again   b
when you say that a man refuses to do what he knows to be
good, overcome by the pleasure of the moment.

' "The absurdity will become clear if we give up using
several words at the same time – pleasant, painful, *good*
(*agathon*), bad (*kakon*) – and since they amount to only two
things, let us call them by two names: first of all, good and
evil (*kakon*), and then pleasure and pain. Making this substitution let us say that the man, knowing bad for what it   c
is, still does it. But if someone asks why, we shall say:
'Because he is overcome.' 'By what?' he will ask us. But it
will no longer be possible for us to say 'By pleasure': for
another word has been substituted for pleasure – the good.

The Protagoras

So let us now say in reply that he has been overcome. . .
'By what?' he will say. . . 'By the good,' we shall reply, 'by
Zeus!' And if our questioner turns out to be rude, he will
d   laugh and say: 'How ludicrous to suggest someone does
something bad knowing it to be bad, when there is no need
to do it, because he has been overcome by the good! Is this,'
he will say, 'because the good proves not to outweigh the
bad in you, or because it does?' Obviously we shall reply
that 'It does not'; otherwise the man whom we say was
overcome by pleasure would not have gone astray. 'But in
virtue of what,' he will say, 'can it be said that the bad
outweighs the good or the good the bad? Can it be in virtue
e   of anything other than the fact that the one is greater and
the other smaller? Or because the one is more and the other
less?' We shall be unable to offer any alternative. 'So obviously,' he will say, 'by being overcome you mean choosing
greater *ills* (*kaka*) in preference to lesser good.' So far so
good.
  ' "Now let us go back and substitute the words '*pleasant
(hēdu)*' and '*painful (aniaron)*' in the same propositions:
where before we said that a man does something bad, let us
now say that he does what is painful, knowing it to be
356a painful, overcome by pleasure, although obviously the
pleasure does not outweigh the pain. And surely the only
way in which pleasure can fail to outweigh the pain must
lie in their relative excess or deficiency? That is, in their
being mutually greater or smaller, more or less, stronger or
weaker. Now if someone says: 'But there is all the difference,
Socrates, between immediate and postponed pleasure and
pain,' I should say: 'Not, surely, a difference of anything
other than pleasure and pain?' For it cannot involve any-
b   thing else. So like a man who is good at weighing, take all
the pleasures together, and all the pains together, and making allowance in the scales for their relative proximity or
distance, tell us which is greater. Thus if you are weighing
pleasures against pleasures it is always the more and the
greater which must be chosen; but if you are weighing pain
against pain, the less and smaller is to be preferred; if,
however, you are weighing pleasure against pain, then if
the pleasure outweighs the pain, be this a case of the more

58

distant outweighing the more immediate or *vice versa*, then
we must undertake that action which entails that pleasure;
but if the pleasure is outweighed by the pain, we must not   c
undertake it. Could it possibly be otherwise," I should say.
I know they could not disagree.'

To this he agreed.

' "That being so, answer me this," I shall say: "Do not
some sizes appear larger from close up and smaller from a
distance when you look at them?" They will agree. And
similarly for width and quantity; and the same sound seems
louder from nearby and fainter at a distance?" They would
agree. "Well, if doing well depended on our ability in prac-   d
tice to choose the larger and avoid the smaller with respect
to physical size, what would safeguard our lives: the *art of
measurement* (*metrētikē technē*) or the power of appear-
ances over us? Or is it not this power exerted by appearance
which often confuses us and makes us change our minds
back and forth about the same things when we set about
the practical choice between great and small, whereas the
art of measurement would have rendered this illusion pow-
erless and in showing the truth would have kept our minds   e
steadily on the truth without confusion, and thus guarded
our lives?" Would men agree that it is the art of measurement, rather than any other art, which preserves us?'

'The art of measurement,' he agreed.

' "And what about this? Suppose that safety in life depended on our choosing between odd and even, whenever it
was necessary to choose more and whenever it was necessary to choose less, whether independently or relatively, disregarding proximity and distance: what would it be that
preserved our lives? Wouldn't it be *knowledge*? Moreover   357a
would it not be some kind of quantitative knowledge, since
it is a skill concerned with excess and deficiency? And since
we are concerned in particular with odd and even, must not
that knowledge be mathematics?" Would men agree with
us, or not?'

Protagoras agreed that they would.

' "Well then, gentlemen: since it has become clear to us
that our safety in life depends on the correct choice between
pleasure and pain, involving as it does the consideration of

b　　more and less, greater and smaller, nearer and more remote, is not the inquiry in the first place about measurement, since it is concerned with excess, deficiency and equality?" '
'Inevitably.'
' "And since it is quantitative then necessarily, I take it, it is a *skill* (*technē*) and a *science* (*epistēmē*)?" They will agree. "In that case, we shall investigate at some other time the question of what kind of skill or science it is, although the mere fact that it is a science satisfies the requirement
c　　of proof which you asked Protagoras and me to give. Your question, if you remember, arose when Protagoras and I were agreeing that there was nothing stronger than *knowledge* (*epistēmē*), and that wherever knowledge is present, it is always stronger than pleasure or anything else; but you claimed that pleasure is frequently too strong for the man who knows better, and it was at that point, when we were disagreeing with you, that you asked: 'Protagoras and Socrates, if what happens to us in such a case is not that we are overcome by pleasure, then what does happen to us, and what do you say happens to us? Explain.' Now if at that
d　　point we had immediately said that it was ignorance, you would have laughed at us; but if you laugh at us now, you will be laughing at yourselves as well. You have admitted that men go wrong in choosing between pleasure and pain – that is to say, good and bad – because of a deficiency of knowledge; and not only of knowledge but, as you have already agreed, of quantitative knowledge. And you presumably realise that an error brought about by a lack of
e　　knowledge is caused by ignorance. Therefore, that is what being overcome by pleasure is: supreme ignorance. And it is of this ignorance that Protagoras here claims to be the physician, along with Prodicus and Hippias. But you, because of your belief that it is something other than ignorance, refuse to send your sons to these teachers of this subject, these sophists, and refuse to visit them yourselves, on the assumption that it cannot be taught; and because you prefer to hoard your money rather than pay it to them you do badly both individually and as a community."

Section XXIII

Section XXIII

'So much for our reply to the *general public (polloi)*. But 358a
now, Hippias and Prodicus, let me ask you as well as Protagoras this question, so that you can all be involved in the
answers: do you think the view I have expressed is true or
false?'
They all fell over themselves to agree that what had been
said was correct.
'Then you agree,' I said, 'that pleasure is good and pain
is bad. . . . I beg leave to waive Prodicus' semantic distinctions; whether you call it pleasure, or enjoyment, or gratification, or whatever else you prefer to call it, my dear   b
Prodicus, please answer to my intended meaning.'
Prodicus laughed and the others agreed.
'Well then, gentlemen' I said, 'what about this? Are not
all actions which are directed at a pleasant and painless life
admirable (kalon)? And is not an admirable action *good
(agathon)* and *beneficial (ōphelimon)*?'
It was agreed.
'Then if,' I said, 'a pleasure is good and someone knows or
thinks that some course of action open to him is better than
the course of action in which he is engaged, he will never
proceed to the inferior course when he could have adopted   c
the better. Nor can "being overcome by oneself" be anything
other than ignorance or overcoming oneself be anything but
wisdom (sophia).'
They all agreed.
'What now? Do you agree that ignorance is having a false
opinion and being mistaken about matters of importance?'
This too they all agreed.
'Furthermore,' I said, 'nobody willingly goes to face *evil
(kaka)* or what he thinks is *bad (kaka)*, nor is it in human   d
nature, apparently, for a man to seek what he thinks is bad
in preference to the good; and when compelled to choose one
of two *evils*, no one chooses the greater where the less is
open to him?'
We were in complete agreement.
'Very well, then,' I said. 'Do you recognize the existence
of terror and fear, and define it in the same way as I do? I

am addressing myself to you in particular, Prodicus. I define it as the expectation of something bad, whether you call it fear or terror.'

e   Protagoras and Hippias thought this was the definition both of terror and fear, while Prodicus held that it was the definition of terror but not of fear.

'No matter, Prodicus,' I said, 'provided you agree to this: if our former statements are true, no man will be prepared to face a situation which terrifies him when it is open to him to avoid it, will he? Is that not impossible on the basis of the points we have agreed so far? For we have agreed that a man is terrified by what he conceives as bad; and that no man willingly either faces or chooses what he conceives as bad.'

359a   Everyone agreed to that too.

'Then with all these points established, Prodicus and Hippias, how can Protagoras defend the truth of his original reply – and by that I do not mean the first of all, when he said that there were five parts of excellence of which no one was like any other, each having its unique capacity – that's not the statement I mean, but the one he made later, when he said that while four of them were tolerably close to each

b   other, one of them was very different from the rest, namely *courage*, and I should be able, so he claimed, to see the truth of his words in this way: "You will find, Socrates," he said, "men who are utterly unholy, unjust, lawless and ignorant who are nevertheless exceedingly courageous; and from this you will realise that courage is very different from the other parts of excellence."And for my part, even then I was amazed at his reply, though all the more so now, since I have covered all these points with you. I asked him, therefore, if he called courageous men daring, and he said "yes,

c   who readily go to meet what many fear to face." You do remember giving these replies, Protagoras,' I said.

He admitted it.

'Very well,' I said, 'tell me what it is that they readily go to meet: the same thing as cowards?'

'No,' he said.

'Something else then?'

'Yes,' he said.

Section XXIII

'Isn't it true that cowards head for safety while coura-geous men head for *the terrible (ta deina)*?'

'So they say, Socrates.'

'Perfectly true,' I said, 'but that wasn't my question; I d wanted to know what you yourself think the courageous head for. Do they head for *the terrible (to deinon)* in the belief that it is terrible, or for the opposite?'

'Well, on your previous arguments, Socrates, this was shown to be impossible,' he said.

'Right again,' I said. 'If therefore these arguments were sound, no one goes to meet what he conceives to be terrible, since being overcome by oneself was found to be ignorance.'

He conceded this.

'But in that case, everyone, courageous and cowardly alike, heads for whatever makes him feel secure, from which it follows that cowards and courageous men head for the same things.'

'But look here, Socrates,' he said, 'the coward and the e courageous man head for completely opposite things: for example, courageous men are willing to go to war, the cow-ards are not.'

'And do they do so,' I said, 'because they consider war to be *admirable (kalon)* or because they consider it *contempt-ible (aischron)*?'

'Oh, admirable,' he said.

'And has not our previous discussion committed us to the view that if it is admirable it must be *good (agathon)*? For we agreed that all admirable deeds are also good.'

'What you say is true,' he said, 'and I still hold that view.'

'Quite right too,' I said. 'But which group is it that you 360a claim do not wish to go to war, although it is admirable and good?'

'The cowards,' he said.

'And if it is admirable and good,' I said, 'is it also *desirable (hēdu)*?'

'Well, that's what we've agreed,' he said.

'And are the cowards consciously unwilling to make for what is more admirable and better and more desirable?'

'By admitting that we shall be completely destroying our previously agreed conclusions' he said.

63

'What about the man of courage? Does he not make for what is more admirable and better and more desirable?'

'I must necessarily concede the point.'

b   'Then all in all, isn't it true that the courageous are not susceptible to *contemptible* (*aischroi*) fears, when they do feel fear, nor do they derive their sense of security, when they do feel safe, from anything which is contemptible?'

'Correct,' he said.

'If not contemptible, then *admirable* (*kala*)?'

He conceded the point.

'And if admirable, then also good?'

'Yes.'

'And is it not true that the cowardly and the daring and the mad are on the contrary susceptible to contemptible fears and derive their sense of security from what is contemptible?'

He conceded the point.

'And do they thus feel secure in what is contemptible and bad through anything but untutored *ignorance* (*amathia*)?'

'No, they don't,' he said.

c   'Well then,' I said, 'this thing which makes cowards cowardly, do you call it courage or cowardice?'

'I would say, cowardice,' he said.

'But has it not emerged that they are cowards in virtue of their ignorance of what is *terrible*?'

'Certainly,' he said.

'So they are cowards in virtue of this kind of ignorance?'

He conceded the point.

'And you have admitted that what makes them cowards is cowardice?'

He agreed.

'Then wouldn't ignorance of what is and is not terrible be cowardice?'

He nodded.

'But now,' I said, 'courage is the opposite of cowardice,'

d   He agreed.

'And is not the *knowledge* (*sophia*) of what is and is not terrible the opposite of ignorance of those things?'

Here too he nodded.

'But ignorance of these things is cowardice?'

64

Section XXIV

With great reluctance, once again, he nodded.

'Therefore *knowledge* (*sophia*) of what is and is not terrible is *courage*, whose opposite is the ignorance of these things?'

By now he was no longer prepared even to nod, and sat silent. So I said:

'Protagoras, why don't you answer my question, yes or no?'

'Finish the job yourself,' he said.

'I have only one question left to ask you,' I said. 'Are you   e
still of the opinion that there are some people who are utterly *ignorant* (*amathēs*) yet very courageous?'

'You seem utterly determined to get your way and have me giving the answers, Socrates,' he said. 'Still if it makes you happy. I shall say that on the basis of what we have agreed, I do consider this impossible.'

Section XXIV

'But my only motive for this whole line of questioning,' I said, 'has been my desire to investigate the general subject of excellence, and what excellence itself is. For I know that once this matter has been clarified, we shall be best able to   361a
settle the truth of the question which gave rise to this whole lengthy discussion; I refer to my claim that excellence is not teachable, and yours that it is teachable. And it seems to me that the outcome of our discussion is like someone pointing an accusing finger and laughing; and could he but speak he would say: "What a pair you are, Socrates and Protagoras! You, Socrates, who were originally maintaining that excellence is not teachable, are now eagerly turning yourself inside out attempting to prove that all things are know-   b
ledge, including justice, moderation and courage, which would make it obvious that excellence must be teachable. For if excellence were anything other than knowledge, as Protagoras was attempting to maintain, it obviously could not be teachable; but now, if it turns out to be entirely a

65

matter of knowledge, as you are so eager to maintain, Socrates, it would be amazing if it were not teachable. But Protagoras, on the other hand, after committing himself to the view that it is teachable, is now apparently rushing off to the opposite extreme and trying to show it to be almost

c   anything rather than knowledge, in which case it could not possibly be teachable." So when I survey this terrible confusion and chaos, Protagoras, I have a burning desire to make sense of it. And I would like us to give a thorough account of this subject until we can emerge with an understanding of what excellence is, and only then return to attack the question of whether it can or cannot be taught. For otherwise I am afraid that old Epimetheus [After-

d   thought] may lead us into many errors in our inquiry, just as he was negligent toward us in your story, when he allotted the various capacities. I must say I preferred Prometheus [Forethought] to Epimetheus in the story. For I am making use of him, and taking forethought for my entire life when I concern myself with all these questions. And as I said at the beginning, I should much prefer to investigate the question with your help, should you be willing.'

To which Protagoras replied:

'For my part, Socrates, I admire both your enthusiasm

e   and skill with arguments. I do not regard myself as a bad man, certainly not one to be envious of others. For I have often spoken of you, since of all those I have met, particularly those of your generation, you are the man I most admire; and let me say that I should not be surprised if you became one of the great men of *wisdom* (*sophia*). Let us indeed return to our examination of these questions on some other occasion, whenever you please. But now it is about time to turn to something else.'

362a   'As you please,' I said. 'As a matter of fact the time of the appointment I mentioned is long gone; I only stayed behind to please the noble Callias.'

Having said and heard these things, we went away.

Commentary

Section I (309a–310a)

1. Is this not an odd way for a philosophical work to begin? What form would you expect a philosophical work to take?

   i. From what type of work would you expect the kind of opening which Plato gives?

  ii. What good reasons are there for casting a philosophical work in dramatic form?

2. What is the single quality which attracts Socrates both to Alcibiades and to Protagoras?

3. Why is Protagoras said to be superior to Alcibiades in this respect?

4. Is it fair to compare mental with physical beauty as Socrates does here?

   i. Is it possible to speak of 'mental' beauty at all? The Greek word for beautiful (*kalos*) can be used either in the sense of 'attractive to the senses' or as a virtual synonym for good (*agathos*), or again to mean 'fine' or 'noble'. In this last meaning *kalos* is as reminiscent of the period of aristocratic rule in ancient Greece, as our word 'noble' is of our own aristocratic age. The Greek aristocrat was originally a military leader; his most admired attribute was his physical prowess, and, as an outward manifestation of his strength, beauty. Even when this dialogue was written, at the beginning of the fourth century B.C., with the Athenian democracy a century old, those of aristocratic de-

67

Commentary

scent were still referred to as the *kaloi k'agathoi* – the beautiful and good. But while physical beauty was no longer the mark of the most respected men in society, the word *kalos* retained its implication of good (*agathos*), which the Greeks associated with the ability to succeed at least as much as with what we call 'virtue'. At the same time mental powers and skills or expert knowledge were becoming correspondingly more highly esteemed. The word *kalos* (with *agathos* one of the two most important terms of commendation in the Greek language) applied to any person, act or thing which was regarded as attractive or worthy of admiration and esteem. Is attractiveness absolute, or does it vary in relation to the qualities people happen to regard as important at a particular time?

5. Socrates says that he finds the prospect of conversation with a reputedly wise man more compelling than the company of his friend Alcibiades. Evidently his belief that wisdom is finer than physical beauty is, for him, no mere theory. What qualities make mental beauty the more beautiful? Is the comparison of mental and physical beauty possible only because of the ambiguous meaning of *kalos*? Or could it be argued that goodness and nobility are finer than physical beauty regardless of what language we use?

6. Consider Plato's characterisation of Socrates. Why, in this dialogue, is Plato concerned to establish the personality of Socrates in our imagination?

   i. Clearly the *Protagoras* is not only an abstract philosophical treatise but also a dramatic work. Plato therefore uses the techniques of the dramatist – plot development, thematic development and characterisation – to make his ideas more vivid. Is he in danger of diverting the reader's attention from those ideas to less important dramatic elements?

Section II

7. If someone told you that Protagoras was wise, what questions would you want to ask him about Protagoras?

   i. For instance, if someone told you that Alcibiades was beautiful, would that tell you what he looked like? What else would you need to know before you could pick him out in a crowd? What would you want to know before you could tell whether you also thought him beautiful?

Section II (310a–311a)

1. What sort of young man is Hippocrates? What details does Plato give to create this characterisation?

2. Hippocrates complains that Protagoras is not making him wise. What does the tone of Socrates' response – that Protagoras will make him wise for a fee – suggest about Socrates' true opinion of Protagoras?

3. Hippocrates has attributed two slightly different qualities to Protagoras: the first as his own opinion, the second as the opinion of everyone else. What quality does he think he will acquire if he buys what Protagoras has to sell?

4. From this exchange between Hippocrates and Socrates, is it possible to tell what Protagoras' profession is?

5. If Hippocrates told you that Protagoras was wise, what questions would you, as his guardian, wish to ask him about Protagoras?

   i. Hippocrates obviously believes that Protagoras is wise. What does he hope to gain from this wisdom?

   ii. Is wisdom something that can be learned?

Commentary

iii. The Greek word *sophos* (wise) and its abstract noun *sophia* (wisdom) have a wider application than our word 'wise'. Not only was a *sophos* a sage or wise old man, but skilled artists and craftsmen were called *sophos* in virtue of a skill (*technē*) which required intelligence or knowledge (*epistēmē*) or technical facility. Correspondingly *sophia* may involve either wisdom as we understand the word, or, more commonly, knowledge (as at 360d), or 'know-how'. Does this affect your answers to (i) and (ii)?

6. What is Socrates' real motive for saying that he wishes to wait for a while and chat before going to Callias' house?

   i. What is Socrates' personal attitude toward Hippocrates? What are their respective ages?

Section III (311a–312b)

1. What does Socrates wish to know about Protagoras?

   i. Socrates seems to be asking merely what Hippocrates thinks he will be getting for his money. If Socrates had asked instead 'Of what does his wisdom consist?' he might perhaps be asking a more important and interesting question. Why, then, does he start his questioning of Hippocrates on so simple and unphilosophical an issue as this?

   ii. Socrates first asks Hippocrates, in effect, what it is about Protagoras that makes the young man willing to spend so much money on him, and what he hopes to become as result. In the light of what Hippocrates has already said about Protagoras, what would he have answered to that question?

   iii. Instead of letting him reply at once, Socrates elaborates the question with a series of examples. What difference do these examples make to the answer Hippocrates can now give?

2. In spite of Hippocrates' reluctance to accept this conclusion, could he fairly have denied it?

   i. Hippocrates has to admit that his wish to study with Protagoras, who is known as a 'sophist', implies that he too wishes to be a sophist. What is it about the wording of the previous questions that forces him to make this admission?

   ii. Socrates' examples all take the form '*x* is an *A*; therefore you study with *x* to become an *A*. Is this connection of what a person does professionally and what is learned from him a valid one? Can you think of any other reason for paying a plumber to teach you plumbing than to become a plumber yourself? But if you pay someone as a professional violin teacher, does this mean that you too want to be able to earn money by teaching the violin?

3. When Hippocrates admits that, by the logic of the argument, he wishes to study with Protagoras to become a sophist, he blushes. Why?

   i. Here are some possible reasons. What support is there in the text for each of them?
   (a) He is angry because he thinks that Socrates has tricked him into admitting something which he did not really mean.
   (b) He is embarrassed because he now realises that he does not really know for what purpose he wants Protagoras' lessons.
   (c) He does not wish to be a sophist at all, but thinks that the training of the sort Protagoras offers will give him a valuable education.
   (d) There is something disreputable about the desire to be a sophist.

71

4. In the light of the text so far, what does a sophist seem to be?

Section IV (312b–313a)

1. Hippocrates first defines a sophist as 'someone who has knowledge of wise things'. Why is Socrates not satisfied with this answer?

2. Socrates' next question is again introduced by examples from the skilled professions. We may doubt whether he is correct to assume that wisdom consists solely of specialist skill and knowledge. In the light of the meaning of *sophos* (see II.5.iii), is Socrates' insistence that a man must be *sophos about something* correct? Can a person be wise without specialist skills and knowledge?

    i.   For what do we value wisdom?

    ii. If you wanted to buy a racehorse, whose advice would you prefer, the wise man's or that of the expert in horses? But if you wished to know whether it was right to violate a law which you considered unjust, whose opinion would you ask: a lawyer's or a 'wise man's'?

    iii. If expert knowledge does not automatically confer wisdom, how are the two connected?

3. So far Socrates has employed two methods of questioning Hippocrates:
    (a) He asks questions which preclude all but a limited range of answers (see 311b–312a and III.1.i–iii).
    (b) He persistently refuses to be satisfied by the answer given, asking instead for an explanation of the answer itself – as in the present case.

    Is this way of questioning someone fair?

Section IV

i. Would it be fair in a law court?

ii. Would it be a fair way to interview a public figure?

iii. Whether it is fair or not, why does Socrates use it here?

4. What is Socrates' motive in pointing out that Hippocrates' answer – that a sophist knows how to produce clever speakers – is possibly true but not sufficient?

    i. Although Hippocrates has told Socrates what a sophist knows how to do, he has not told him what a sophist knows. How does the analogy of the lyre-player help to make this distinction?

    ii. Are there any professions whose practitioners are thought of as clever speaker by Hippocrates' standards but not by Socrates' standards?

5. In the aristocratic era of ancient Greece young men were brought up on Homeric epic, full of examples of courage, endurance, piety to the gods and sound leadership. In practical terms their training was predominantly military and physical. Their education, therefore, trained them to give military leadership and to govern the rest of society from a position of aristocratic privilege. When, however, we find that in the fifth century B.C. there were teachers and students of 'the art of clever speaking', we may infer that a major social and political change had taken place. This change was the emergence in Athens, during the first half of the fifth century, of a radically democratic constitution such as the world has not seen since.

    The best ancient picture of the history and working of the Athenian political system is Aristotle's *Constitution of Athens*. For our purposes these general points will help to clarify the position of the sophists and the motives of young men like Hippocrates. To be a citizen of Athens was to be a politician, since, if you were a free adult male of Athenian parents, you were entitled to speak and vote in the legislative assembly (*ekklēsia*).

73

Commentary

No law could be passed, no major executive decision taken, unless it had been passed by the people (*dēmos*) in the *ekklēsia*. The magistrates were elected each year and could only administer, not initiate policy. The citizens therefore reigned supreme, so that if a man wished to gain political influence or to carry through a policy, he had to secure the support of the *dēmos* and convince them that his policy was in their best interest.

Why does Hippocrates wish to acquire the art of clever speaking?

6. As the influence of the democratic constitution became increasingly apparent, many of the high-born and wealthy Athenians began to think that it was wrong for affairs of state to be in the hands of the uneducated and irresponsible masses. Surely, many of them argued, the complex business of governing should be in the hands of men best fitted to the task by breeding, education and administrative ability. Moreover their dissatisfaction was tinged with growing bitterness. For, as they saw it, radical democratic politicians, in pursuit of political prestige, were victimising them in order to ingratiate themselves with the masses. Not only did the wealthy feel burdened with extra taxes, but they were frequently prosecuted and fined by men whom they regarded as ambitious politicians with no scruples about playing on the jealousy which the poor feel toward the rich.

There were no judges in an Athenian court; the jury, drawn by lot from those citizens who presented themselves for selection on that day, not only determined guilt or innocence, but in most cases also set the penalty. Moreover the jurors were paid a fee for jury-service – in fact the equivalent of a labourer's daily wage. Consequently those presenting themselves for jury duty were often the poor and unemployed who, at least in the opinion of the rich, were all the more likely to deal harshly with a wealthy aristocratic defendant. After all, the wealthy argued, members of the jury had a vested interest in fining the rich or exiling them and sequestering their property, since the proceeds would pass to

74

the ownership of the state, which was controlled by the very *dēmos* who made up the juries.

This picture of the Athenian legal system overemphasises its potential as a battlefield in a class struggle. It would be a mistake to see the Athenian juries merely as kangaroo courts against the *kaloi k'agathoi*. But this is just how the democracy appeared to many members of the Athenian upper class. Proceedings in court consisted of one speech for the prosecution and one for the defence in public cases and two on each side in private actions. All speeches were limited in time, during which both sides could produce witnesses or their written testimony. Since there was no cross-examination of witnesses and no impartial judge's summary, both sides depended for their success on swaying the emotions of the jury in their favour, and many litigants not themselves trained in oratory hired professional speechwriters. Therefore rhetorical training – the art of clever speaking – became the central study of a well-born young man's education. In both *ekklēsia* and law court the ability to adapt one's argument to the known prejudices and self-interest of the audience might count for as much as the merits of one's case. This system, which placed greater value on intellectual qualities than on hereditary position and wealth, led to the emergence of the sophists, teachers of the rhetorical techniques suited to the needs of Athenian political life. Their teaching methods consisted of training their students to argue convincingly for both sides of a question in turn.

In an aristocratic society, position and power would be determined by birth. In an oligarchy they would be determined largely by wealth. In democratic Athens political power would be determined by . . . what?

7. Why might Socrates be concerned about the moral effect of such a course of instruction on the mind of the young and impressionable Hippocrates?

Commentary
Section V (313a–314c)

1. The Greek word *psuchē* embraces all the non-physical aspects of a person, including the intellectual and the spiritual. How might Hippocrates' *psuchē* be in danger from learning to speak cleverly?

    i. Socrates draws an analogy between the purchase and consumption of food and drink from travelling salesmen and the purchase and consumption of courses of instruction from travelling sophists. Food, when it enters the body, changes the body, promotes or inhibits its growth, makes it stronger or weaker, more healthy or less healthy. When, earlier, Socrates said 'But now that something is at stake which you consider more important than your body – your mind – by which your entire welfare is determined, depending on whether your mind turns out good or bad. . .', what quality of mind did he mean? How can this quality be made better or worse by a course in clever speaking?

    ii. Would courses of instruction (*mathēmata*) which consisted solely in training the student to manipulate arguments irrespective of the merits of the case be a useful course for a politically ambitious young man? What qualities would Socrates consider endangered by such a course?

    iii. If, on the other hand, Protagoras' course purports to teach his students how to present sound judgments based on knowledge, can it succeed unless it also teaches the students how to form sound judgments in the first place?

    iv. Is it possible to teach how to form sound judgments about a subject without teaching the subject itself?

2. What will Socrates need to find out about Protagoras in order to establish whether the courses of instruction which he has for sale are safe to buy?

Section V

    i. A man with medical knowledge understands what constitutes physical health, and so can distinguish which foods are good for the body and which are bad. What knowledge does a man need in order to distinguish between good and bad courses of instruction?

3. While we are being educated we develop three facets of the mind: we acquire both knowledge and mental skills, and we develop our values. Insofar as what we learn is related to practical and political matters, we may say that education makes a man an effective member of his society. But can we tell, solely on the basis of his knowledge and skills, whether he is socially useful?

    i. Are the knowledge of atomic physics and the skill to apply that knowledge socially desirable in themselves, irrespective of the ends towards which they are directed?

    ii. Can we say that legal or political knowledge and skills are socially desirable in themselves? Is the lawyer or politician a good member of society, irrespective of the ends towards which his skills are directed?

    iii. If the knowledge and skills being taught have moral or social implications, does it follow that the teacher has a duty also to educate a student's social and moral understanding? Would this amount to indoctrination?

4. Socrates has been probing Hippocrates' reasons for visiting Protagoras. He has achieved his purpose when Hippocrates, in confusion, says: 'Oh dear, now I have nothing I can say.' Why, then, does Plato make Socrates follow this with an emotional harangue?

    i. What does the emotional tone of 313a–314c show about Socrates' concern for Hippocrates?

    ii. Is Socrates visiting Protagoras because he is per-

Commentary

sonally interested in the issues which his discussion with Hippocrates has raised; or is he concerned for Hippocrates' moral welfare?

Section VI (314c–316a)

1. After introducing Protagoras, Plato quickly diverts our attention first to his followers, then to the other two sophists and finally to the general scene at Callias' house. Why does Plato concentrate on description here rather than move directly to a confrontation between Socrates and Protagoras?

   i. How does the description of Protagoras' followers colour our impression of the man himself?

   ii. Plato introduces both Prodicus and Hippias with quotations from the same passage in Homer (*Odyssey* 11. 563–635), in which Odysseus in the underworld catches sight of the great demigods. How does this colour our impression of these two men?

   iii. From the details of Callias' house – the doorkeeper's reluctance to admit more sophists, the improvised guest room, and Plato's list of the people there – what is the atmosphere of this scene?

   iv. Of what literary form are the descriptive techniques used here characteristic?

2. If Protagoras, Hippias and Prodicus were to describe their opinions of the proper relationship between teacher and student, what would they say?

   i. For these three sophists, what is the purpose of going to a teacher?

   ii. Considering his earlier conversation with Hippocrates, what is Socrates' opinion of the function of the teacher and of his relationship with the student?

iii. What points for and against both views of teaching can you make?

3. Instead of beginning at once with his philosophical subject-matter, Plato has presented three introductory scenes: first a dialogue between Socrates and an unnamed friend, then a conversation with Hippocrates, and finally a description of the scene at Callias' house. Why has he done this?

   i. Compare the function of each scene. To what extent is each concerned with (a) philosophical issues, (b) characterisation and (c) setting the dialogue in a realistic scene?

   ii. Although Protagoras has not yet spoken, Plato has given a lot of information about him.
   (a) What do you know about him as a fact?
   (b) What is the attitude of Callias' guests toward him? Are they all there for the same reason?
   (c) What is your attitude toward Protagoras?

   iii. You are probably more sceptical about Protagoras than his admirers. How have these introductory scenes created this separation between you and the audience in the dialogue?

4. To what ends can a dramatist exploit the device of an audience both within his work and external to it – an actual audience and a fictional one?

   i. By way of comparison, consider Shakespeare's use of this technique in *A Midsummer Night's Dream* or *Hamlet*.

5. Callias' guests exist in the world of the late 430s B.C. when popular democracy was strong and confident, Athens at the height of her power and Sophism a new and vigorous intellectual movement. The audience for whom

Commentary

Plato wrote the dialogue was living thirty to forty years later, after the military disasters and violent political upheavals of the end of the fifth century which culminated in Athens' capitulation to Sparta in 403/2 B.C. The defeat was followed by an imposed and repressive oligarchic regime, some leaders of which had been associated both with the sophists and with Socrates. Indeed, some of these are present in the company at Callias' house. After the overthrow of this regime and the restoration of the democracy, Socrates was tried on a charge of irreligion and corrupting youth, and was executed in 399 B.C. Clearly there are differences of historical circumstance and political outlook between the fictional audience of the 430s and Plato's intended audience of the 390s. What are they?

Section VII (316a–317e)

1. At 316c Protagoras thanks Socrates for showing a very proper consideration. In what way is Socrates' question 'considerate'?

   i. What, according to Socrates, is now Hippocrates' object in coming to Protagoras?

   ii. Considering 312a, 313c–314c and Protagoras' own remarks at 316c–d, why does Socrates suggest that his business might best be handled with discretion?

2. What does Protagoras mean by the 'sophistic art'?

   i. We have already seen that sophists have two main characteristics: they are, or claim to be, wise; and they teach. In ancient times artists, especially poets, had a special position which they lack today. For, in the first place, they were often thought to have, *via* the Muses, a divine inspira-

80

tion, and tended, as result, to be regarded as repositories of religious, ethical and even political wisdom. When Homer writes 'Sing, Muse, of the wrath of Achilles', this is not, as it would be today, only a poetic conceit. Indeed Homer's epics were held in something of the same reverence as many people have for the Bible. Moreover poetry had a special role in education, as the medium through which the received traditions, beliefs and aspirations of a community could be instilled in the young. Apart from the 'three R's', traditional education consisted mainly in the study of great works of the past.

In equating the sophists with traditional artists, what impression of sophists is Protagoras trying to give?

ii. When he calls poets, seers and physical trainers sophists, is Protagoras using the word 'sophist' as a synonym for 'teacher'? If so, then why does he think that these people have had to conceal their true intent from the rest of society?

iii. What effect does Protagoras intend to have on his listeners when he claims that he, unlike past 'sophists', neither resorts to façades nor tries unsuccessfully to escape the opprobrium of the rest of society?

iv. Ever since Thales, at the beginning of the sixth century B.C., philosophers had been inquiring into the nature of the universe and of matter. In the second half of the fifth century scientific speculation took on new momentum, while the critical intellects of philosophers turned increasingly to the nature and foundations of morality. In 423 B.C. the Athenian playwright Aristophanes produced a comedy, the *Clouds*, in which he satirised this movement. It provides not only a useful picture of the scope of sophistic activities, but also an insight into the sources of popular suspicion and even prejudice against them. In the play we find them (or rather, ironically, Socrates!) indulging in preposterous scientific experiments and in speculations in geometry, geography and astronomy. More sinister, they deny the existence of the traditional gods, daring to suggest, for example, that storms are caused not by the anger of a god but by purely meteorological phenomena.

Protagoras himself may have been expelled from Athens for writing a book, *On the Divine*, which begins: 'Whether there be gods or no, and what they are like, I cannot tell.' Together with religious scepticism went moral scepticism. Justification was demanded for ideas of justice and virtue which had been accepted for centuries. Critias, who appears in this scene, was, in later life, to make a character in a play say that justice was invented by rulers wishing to impose order on their citizens and that religion itself was a political fiction designed to intimidate citizens into conformity even in their private lives [Diels. 88.25; Ferguson and Chisholm pp. 197–8]. At the same time there was a growing awareness of the variety of political and judicial institutions under which the various Greek *poleis* were governed, and of the range of often mutually contradictory ethical codes to be observed in the Hellenic and Barbarian worlds. This awareness, sharpened as it must have been by the wide circulation of Herodotus' encyclopaedic *History*, eventually led many intellectuals to question whether any one system of values could be regarded as the right one.

How, then, do the concerns of artists as described in (i) and of sophists differ in such a way as to occasion the general acceptance of the former but hostility to the latter?

v. Does the artist impart a special kind of inspired

truth about the world, distinct from empirical or
scientific truth; or does he create a purely aes-
thetic object bearing no relation to truth?

3. Largely because our knowledge of the sophists is derived
   mainly from the testimony of those who, like Plato,
   disapproved of what they were doing, we have come to
   think of the 'sophist' as a smooth-tongued trickster. Correspondingly, we think of a 'sophistical' argument as
   one which seeks, by means of a devious process of
   reasoning, to gain acceptance of a conclusion which
   would otherwise have been held to be obviously erro-
   neous. Such arguments have two main characteristics.
   First, they must start from assumptions which anybody
   would accept as true. Secondly, they present and inter-
   pret those assumptions in such a way that the otherwise
   unacceptable conclusion appears to follow inevitably.
   What features of this speech could be described as
   'sophistical'?

   i. From what we have learned of the 'sophistic art'
      so far, is 'traditional' a likely description of it?

   ii. Does Protagoras deny that sophists engage in any
       of the activities which render them suspect?

4. Does the tone of Protagoras' reply suggest that he is
   really indifferent whether he speaks in public or in
   private?

5. Protagoras has so far been introduced in two ways: first
   he was discussed by Socrates and Hippocrates; here he
   has been described, with some satirical humour, in his
   habitat. What does this speech add to our impression of
   Protagoras' character?

Commentary
Section VIII (317e–319a)

1. Socrates' question at 318a sounds like a simple request for information about Protagoras' course of study. But in the light of what we already know about Socrates' concern in visiting Protagoras, what do we understand him to mean when he asks, on Hippocrates' behalf, 'what the outcome of his studies will be'?

2. Protagoras initially says that Hippocrates will become a better man by associating with him. In what ways could this statement be understood?

    i. Does Protagoras mean that as a result of studying with him Hippocrates will become more capable at something, or that his character will be improved?

    ii. Judging by his comparison of Protagoras with other teachers of skills, how does Socrates affect to understand him?

3. What is Protagoras claiming to teach at 318d–319a?

    i. He contrasts his own course with technical subjects like geometry and astronomy. Is this because what he teaches is not in itself a branch of knowledge, or because unlike these his subject has a direct practical use for ambitious young Athenians?

    ii. What qualities are necessary if a man is to be suitably qualified for conducting the affairs of the city on the one hand, but successful at getting into a position of being able to conduct them on the other?

4. Socrates summarises Protagoras' description of what he teaches as 'citycraft'. Is this an accurate summary of what Protagoras said?

    i. The Greek, *politikē technē*, here rendered as

84

Section VIII

'citycraft', is often translated as 'the art of politics'. But this English translation connotes the activities of professional politicians and the operations of modern political institutions. The word *technē* means 'skill' or 'craft'. (Note, therefore, the mischievous irony in Socrates' suggestion that Protagoras teaches a *technē*, although Protagoras has just pointedly denied it.) The adjective *politikē* is derived from polis, meaning 'a city'. The verb *politeuesthai* means either 'to be a citizen' or 'to take part in the running of a city'. (You will recall from IV.5 that these two were less distinct to the fifth-century Athenian than they are to us.) *Politēs* means 'a citizen'. Thus *politikē* means, roughly, 'having to do with the *polis*', and *politikē technē* is 'the craft related to the *polis*'. What, then, is citycraft?

ii. Is citycraft likely to be a skill which can be analysed and then taught?

5. In the *Dissoi Logoi*, a work often attributed to a follower (or followers) of Protagoras, and on which Plato may have been drawing when he composed this dialogue, we find this:

'And in the first place, will not the man who knows the nature of all things inevitably be able to teach the city to act correctly in all things? And again, the man who knows the skills (*technai*) of speech will also know how to speak correctly on all matters. For if a man is to speak correctly he must speak about what he knows. . . But also if a man is to speak correctly he must understand the things on which he speaks and correctly teach the city to do those things which are good and prevent the city from doing those which are bad. . . ' (Diels 90.8.2–6).

What do you think Protagoras actually included in his curriculum?

6. Protagoras agrees that teaching citycraft is the same as teaching a man to be a good citizen (*agathos politēs*). Is this in fact what you understood by citycraft?

85

Commentary

i. Socrates' original statement, in private, introduced Hippocrates as wishing to become not so much a good as a leading citizen. What is the difference between the qualities we would expect to find in each, and how would this difference affect the type of instruction designed to produce them?

ii. In the light of Socrates' earlier conversation with Hippocrates, why might Socrates wish to shift the focus of Protagoras' statement from the issue of skill at government to that of being a good citizen?

7. Protagoras earlier promised to make Hippocrates better, to which Socrates responded, 'Yes, but a better ... what?' Now Protagoras has agreed that his course has a moral effect: it will make the student a better citizen. What questions would you now like to ask Protagoras?

Section IX (319a–320c)

1. Are Socrates' arguments intended as a systematic refutation of Protagoras' claim to teach excellence? Or does he merely want to encourage Protagoras to pursue the conversation they have started?

i. Is Socrates' manner aggressive, critical or respectful?

ii. Is the style of Socrates' argument that of rigorous logic or of relaxed conversation?

iii. In the *Dissoi Logoi* we find:

'There is a certain proposition, which is neither true nor original, to the effect that wisdom and excellence can be neither taught nor learned. Those who advance this proposition adduce the following arguments: that if you pass a thing on to somebody else, you could not retain it yourself, since it is a single thing; secondly,

86

Section IX

that if it could be taught there would be recognised
teachers of it, as is the case with poetry; thirdly, that
the wise men in Greece would have taught their own
craft to their own families; fourthly, that some already
have attended sophists to no avail; fifthly, that many
have distinguished themselves without attending sophists' (Diels 90.6.1–6).

What does the fact that two of Socrates' arguments are well-known arguments suggest about
his intentions in putting them forward?

iv. 'A degree in politics or ethics does not make a
statesman or a saint, any more than a degree in
English literature makes a man a poet.' Is this an
accurate summary of what Socrates is saying?
What is it that is needed which formal knowledge
and teachable skills do not provide?

2. Socrates argues first that the Athenians, who ought to
know, act as though they consider citycraft unteachable.
He makes two factual claims:
(a) On technical matters involving expert knowledge,
the Athenians allow only recognised experts to contribute advice.
(b) On matters related to the general conduct of the
city's affairs, the Athenians do not expect technical
expertise.
Does it follow that the Athenians do this because they
do not regard citycraft as a teachable skill?

i. Consider the following argument:
Assumption A: If the Athenians think that some
subject can be taught, then they
do not allow everyone to contribute advice about it in the
ekklēsia.
Assumption B: On the subject of the conduct of
the city's affairs (citycraft) *it is
not the case that* the Athenians do
not allow everyone to contribute
advice about it in the *ekklēsia*.

Commentary

> *Conclusion C*: The Athenians consider that the excellence of citycraft is not a thing which can be taught.

This is an instance of a familiar logical operation. For example:

> *Assumption A*: All Dalmatians are members of the canine species.
>
> *Assumption B*: It is not the case that Felix is a member of the canine species.
> _____
>
> *Conclusion C*: Felix is not a Dalmatian.

Is Socrates' reasoning therefore irresistible?

ii. Suppose Protagoras were to paraphrase Socrates' *Assumption A* as follows:

Assumption A_1: If the Athenians think that some subject, x, can be taught, then they allow *only* acknowledged experts at x to contribute advice about x in the *ekklēsia*. (That is, if they allow someone to contribute advice about x, then they consider that he is an expert about x.)

Is there anything to choose between A and A_1? Can Protagoras now accept Socrates' factual statements and deny his conclusions?

iii. To pass from Socrates' *Conclusion C* to the conclusion that citycraft cannot *in fact* be taught, a further assumption is needed (see 319b). Is it an assumption which Protagoras is in a position to dispute?

3. By these arguments, what is it that Socrates says cannot be taught?

i. How are questions related to the general conduct of the city's affairs related to citycraft?

ii. To some extent it is possible for a nuclear physicist to speak with special authority on whether a given policy related to nuclear energy is a feasible means to a given end. Of what would someone have to have expert knowledge if we were to recognise him as able to speak with special authority on how a country should be governed?

iii. Does the common hostility to technocratic or meritocratic forms of government stem from a belief that no technical expert can decide or know what is in our interests? Or does it stem from a reluctance to believe that anything other than democratic appointment could entitle a man to tell us what to do?

4. Socrates points out that although Pericles, the leading statesman of the day, is presumably well-endowed with the excellence of citycraft, he makes no attempt to teach it to his sons. Does this show that the excellence related to citycraft cannot be taught?

i. Recalling what Protagoras claimed to teach at 318e–319a, at what would a leading statesman like Pericles be expert?

ii. In the Athenian democracy a politician's ability to control affairs was derived not from executive powers so much as from influence in the *ekklēsia*. He could only have influence to the extent that the citizens accepted his advice. That is why Thucydides, in a famous passage (*Thuc.* 2.65) said that because of his judgment and prestige Pericles controlled the people by their free consent. If the Athenians regularly accepted his advice, with what excellences must they have deemed him to be endowed?

iii. Hippocrates is going to Protagoras because he wants to become a leading citizen like Pericles (316b–c). This, it seems, involves the ability to give good advice. How are the two things he hoped to learn, the first mentioned at 310d–e, the second at 312b, related to this ability?

Commentary

iv. Socrates lived at a time when it was normal for a
father to pass on his own skills to his sons. His
argument may indicate that this particular excellence is not like other skills. Does it follow from
the fact that something is not a technical subject,
or is not generally taught as part of a regular
curriculum, that it cannot be taught at all?

5. 'He (Pericles) was concerned that Alcibiades might have
a corrupting influence on him (Cleinias)'. (320a) In what
way has Socrates shifted the focus of the argument?

i. In what way did Pericles hope to improve his ward
by sending him to Ariphon?

ii. Some fifteen years after this, in 415 B.C., when
the *ekklēsia* were debating the proposed expedi-
tion against Sicily, Nicias, according to Thucydides, attacked Alcibiades with these words:

'He is too young for his command. He wants to be
admired for the horses he keeps, and because these
things are expensive he wants to make some profit out
of his appointment. Beware of him, and do not give him
the chance of endangering the state in order to live a
brilliant life of his own. Remember, too, that with such
people maladministration of public affairs goes with
personal extravagance.' (*Thuc.* 6.12.2)

In what ways is the influence of Alcibiades likely
to prevent Cleinias acquiring the excellence related to citycraft?

iii. The Greek word *aretē* is often rendered as 'virtue';
but virtue has the connotation of personal morality, often with religious overtones. The *aretē* of a
thing or person is the quality which makes us
value it. We can speak of a good meal or a good
long-distance runner or a good person, where in
each case the word 'good' stands for qualities
which we value; but the goodness of a good meal,
the goodness of the runner and the goodness of
the person are not, of course, the same thing. The

90

Section X

word *aretē*, when applied to a man, stands for whatever qualities are necessary for a man to lead a life which it is valuable to lead, whether these qualities are physical, mental or ethical. We have, therefore, used the word 'excellence' in this translation, thereby avoiding the purely moral and specifically Judaeo-Christian connotations of the word 'virtue'.

Socrates, in introducing this word, has moved the conversation from the consideration of the skills and aptitudes necessary for citycraft to a more general consideration of excellence itself. Would it be possible, nevertheless, to consider the nature of citycraft alone, without considering the wider subject of excellence?

6. Taking Socrates' argument as a whole, what is Protagoras being asked to prove can be taught?

   i. Does Socrates want Protagoras to prove that he can make a man good at politics, good at giving wise and beneficial advice on government, or good in the sense of being a good citizen?

   ii. If Protagoras claims to teach the excellence related to citycraft, can he deny that this must include the study of *aretē* in its more general moral sense?

   iii. Given his awareness of the need for caution (316c–d) would Protagoras be likely to deny it?

7. What points would a detailed reply to Socrates' speech have to cover?

Section X (320c–328d)

[This section covers the whole of Protagoras' long speech. Sections XI and XII treat its two parts in detail.]

Commentary

1. Does this speech sound like an improvised response to Socrates' question?

2. Compare the tone and rhetorical style of Socrates' speech with this speech, especially in the first section – the story.

   i. Protagoras' rather flowery style reflects a change in Plato's Greek. Socrates, so far, has used a more conversational language. Under what circumstances might we expect to hear a more artificial and grandiloquent style of speech than normal discourse requires?

   ii. What are the stylistic differences between the story itself and the subsequent argument?

3. Do both parts of the speech contribute equally to a direct response to Socrates' arguments?

   i. What effect does Protagoras intend the story to have on his audience? How will this influence their evaluation of the rest of the speech?

   ii. Does Protagoras, in the second part of the speech, offer a systematic refutation of Socrates' arguments?

4. Having read the speech through just once, as Protagoras' audience would have heard it just once, can you recall from memory and list all the important points made?

   i. As you read the speech, did Protagoras' arguments seem well-directed and cogent? If so, what are the difficulties in remembering everything he said?

   ii. Does Protagoras intend his audience to be able to remember and analyse each component of his argument when he has completed the entire presentation?

5. Compare Protagoras' method of argument, by long

speech, with Socrates' method of question and answer
which he used with Hippocrates. Which method is better
suited to the presentation of carefully worked-out ideas?
Which is more suited to the exploration of problems to
which the answers are known neither by speaker nor by
listener?

    i. Nearly all Plato's works are in the form of dia-
logues. What does this suggest about Plato's characterisation of Socrates' concerns as a philosopher,
and about his own conception of philosophy?

6. Does Plato intend this speech as a presentation of Protagoras' ideas? Or does he wish to give a demonstration
of effective speaking by a master-sophist?

    i. Protagoras, who, as we have seen, is old enough
to be Socrates' father, appears to have been the
first sophist to travel through Greece charging a
fee for his courses of instruction. The titles of writings which were later attributed to him may well
indicate some of his main concerns: *On Courses of
Instruction, The Art of Debate, On Constitution,
On the Excellences, On Attaining Power, Justice
for a Fee.* His pupil would acquire facility in rhetoric and debate, and expert knowledge in law and
constitutions. He shared Plato's interest in constitutional engineering and drew up the constitution for the Athenian colony of Thurii. But as
a teacher he was particularly associated with the
boast of being able to make the weaker case defeat
the stronger case (Aristotle, *Rhetorica*
B.24.1402a23). His technique was to make his
pupils try to argue with equal persuasiveness on
either side of the same issue. In this he set the
pattern for the sophists who followed him. Critics
such as Aristophanes (who in the *Clouds* levels
the charge at Socrates himself) equated this with
encouraging the young to justify their own injustice by unscrupulously clever argument. Can you

suggest why Plato chose Protagoras as the protagonist of this dialogue?

ii. Given Protagoras' well-known religious scepticism (cf. VII.2.iv), why does Plato make him speak with an air of such conviction on the subject of the divine origin of justice?

iii. Protagoras' most famous doctrine was that 'Man is the measure of all things' (Plato, *Theaetetus* 152a2–4), by which he seems to have meant that since all knowledge must derive from what we experience with the senses, and since sense-experience is subjective or relative to the individual percipient, there can be no such thing as absolute truth or knowledge, but only belief – truth as each person sees it. Consider the consequences of such a position in relation to ethics (see I.4.i). If there is no absolute truth about right and wrong, is justice, for instance, whatever a given individual or society thinks it is?

iv. From the long speech, is it clear whether Protagoras believes in absolute ethical standards or not?

v. Consider these problems: What impression of himself is Protagoras trying to give his audience? From what you know about Socrates, how will he react to this speech? What is your impression now of Protagoras?

Section XI (320c–323a)

1. In the creation story of Genesis the animals were created after man and for his benefit. What does the creation story of Protagoras imply about the relation between man and the other animals?

2. What makes the world of this creation story such that

each creature needs a power for his safety?

   i. In such a world what motivation would underlie all behaviour?

3. What attribute of man does Prometheus' gift of fire represent?

4. Define citycraft as Protagoras uses the word here.

   i. What, in addition to the practical intelligence to make weapons, does a man need in order to be able to conduct war? In what sense is warcraft (*polemikē technē*) a part of citycraft?

   ii. Suppose that these primitives wished to cooperate in warding off wild animals. Each has a different opinion as to who should lead and who should meet the greatest danger. How might citycraft enable them to combine effectively without coming to blows?

   iii. Why are men in their primitive state unable to live in communities without injuring one another?

   iv. Suppose, for example, that they were founding a *polis*. Each would seek to occupy one site most favourable for his own dwelling. How would citycraft enable the resulting conflict to be settled without bloodshed and the collapse of the community?

5. *Dikē* is closely linked to the idea of legal justice. Thus a law court is a *dikastērion*; a juror is a *dikastēs*; *dikē* itself is used for a private lawsuit, while the verb *dikazein* connotes sitting in judgment in a dispute between contending individuals. 'The rule of law' might be a more appropriate rendering of Protagoras' meaning, rather than the more common 'justice' or 'sense of justice'. Sometimes, however, the word has connotations of equity. Thus *dikaios* can mean 'just' in the sense of fair, and *dikaiosunē* can mean justice in its ethical as well as its legal sense.

Commentary

Aidōs is also a difficult idea. It is useless to agree on a code of behaviour if the members of the community do not abide by it. One way in which such conventions are enforced is by public opinion. Members of a community tend to be seriously concerned about the feelings of other members of that community towards them. *Aidōs* represents that fear of public disapproval which ensures that in general we shall follow society's conventions. It is, in effect, what makes us responsive to external moral authority.

Bearing in mind your answer to (4), what ability do the gifts of justice (*dikē*) and a sense of shame (*aidōs*) represent?

    i. The sophist Antiphon in a work *On Truth* says that justice consists in obeying the law, which is a product of agreement and not the codified expression of some moral value (Diels 88.44 Fr. A; Ferguson and Chisholm pp. 129–131). Plato attributes a similar view to the orator Callicles (*Gorgias* 482 c *seq*) and to the sophist Thrasymachus (*Republic* I 338e *seq*.), while much the same view is expressed in the *Sisyphus* by Critias (cf. VII.2.iv) and by Protagoras himself (cf. X.6.iii). When Protagoras says that Zeus gave man *dikē* and *aidōs*, does he mean that Zeus made men able to agree on and conform to whatever laws a society might make, or that he gave them an absolute sense of right and wrong?

    ii. If an individual's sense of what is right conflicts with the dictates of the laws or conventions at that time, ought he to obey his conscience or the law? Is it clear which view Protagoras would take?

6. Does Protagoras' description of the origins of citycraft prove that men think that everyone shares this excellence?

    i. Does Protagoras mean that all men have an equal

share of the skills which are necessary to run a community?

ii. If all men do share citycraft equally, how could Protagoras justify charging high fees for instilling this excellence?

iii. Is Protagoras suggesting that all men share *dikē* and *aidōs* in the sense that they have it from birth or in the sense that all men by living in society inevitably acquire it?

7. Protagoras previously agreed that his course of instruction was citycraft, which, on the evidence of the story, consists of restraints on the pursuit of self-interest for the public good. In the story he says that the origin of this restraint is Zeus' gift of *dikē* and *aidōs*. But at 323a Protagoras uses for 'justice' the word *dikaiosunē* (cf. 5), and for the sense of restraint implied by *aidōs* he now uses *sōphrosunē*, here translated 'moderation', in this context the moral disposition to be law-abiding and restrained in one's personal behaviour towards fellow-citizens. How does this change of emphasis affect the way we understand that all men have the excellence related to citycraft in common?

8. Bearing in mind your discussion of IX.2, has Protagoras shown that Socrates' argument about the behaviour of the Athenian *ekklēsia* was unsound?

Section XII (323a–328d)

How does Protagoras' style of argument differ in this half of the speech?

i. Has the first part of the speech, the story, strictly speaking *proved* that all men share justice and a sense of shame?

Commentary

   ii. In the second part of the speech Protagoras argues both from experience and from analogy. What differences are there between the two methods?

  iii. What are the potential dangers of the two methods?

2. Here are some errors that someone can make in using experience – common sense – or analogy:
   (a) In making an analogy between x and y, the speaker may ignore differences between them which invalidate or outweigh superficial similarities – in other words, the analogy may be false.
   (b) The speaker may describe an experience correctly but it may not prove what he claims it proves.
   (c) The speaker may incorrectly describe an experience; hence, any conclusions he draws from it will be invalid.
   (d) He may assume that because y happens after x, y must be caused by x, a fallacy known as *post hoc propter hoc*. Perhaps something else caused y, not recognised as the cause by the speaker.
   Now consider each of Protagoras' arguments. In each case, has he committed any of these faults? How far does the soundness of each argument depend upon what Protagoras meant by saying that Zeus gave *dikē* and *aidōs* to all men in common (cf. XI.6)?

3. Protagoras says that even a man who knows he is bad will claim to be good, and that this proves that we think that all men share *dikaiosunē*. What other conclusion might be drawn from the same observation?

4. Protagoras argues that punishment is not inflicted for revenge but to deter potential wrongdoers and to reform criminals. Would most people say that the purpose of punishing someone is deterrence or reformation on the one hand, or retribution on the other?

   i. What would most people say if you asked them for an honest opinion about whether the purpose of

98

putting criminals in prison is really deterrence or reformation, or whether it is really retribution or revenge? Would they necessarily give the same answer if you asked which was the better moral justification of punishment?

ii. Protagoras argues that punishment for the sake of revenge is irrational and that the only rational justification for punishment is deterrence or correction. In the light of (i), would you agree?

iii. Is Protagoras justified in using the example of punishment inflicted on wrongdoers to reform them as proof of the teachability of citycraft? For in doing so he seems to assume that what the wrongdoer learns is the same as what the Athenians consider necessary for conducting public affairs. Are they the same?

5. At 325a Protagoras says that the one essential for a state is 'justice, moderation, holiness, or, in short, what I call manly excellence'. What does he mean by saying that these three taken together are 'excellence'?

6. One view of the function of a child's education is that it moulds him – gives him the skills and qualities that society needs and admires. Another view is that education should promote the emotional and intellectual growth and fulfilment of the individual (see V.3). Which of these seems closer to Protagoras' description of education?

i. Which view would Socrates hold?

ii. Consider Protagoras' description of schooling at 325d–326c. Protagoras here stresses the importance of instilling in the young physical and mental harmony (an ideal which we generally associate with 'the Classical'). Which is he saying is more important, moral or intellectual training?

iii. Consider the analogy which Protagoras draws be-

Commentary

tween teaching a young man the law and teaching a child to write (326c–d). In the light of XI.5–6, is Protagoras saying that laws are a rough guide to some absolute ethical standard understood by 'wise men of olden times', or is he saying that learning the law teaches a man to live in a community subject to the rule of law – 'to govern and be governed in accordance with these [laws]' – instead of following 'the random dictates of personal inclination'? In what sense, according to Protagoras, does learning the law make young men better?

7. When Protagoras makes the analogy between the capacity for flute-playing and the capacity for excellence, does he mean that this capacity has its origin in birth, education and upbringing, or in something else?

   i. When, in the story, he described the civilising propensities – *dikē* and *aidōs* – as being given by Zeus and shared by all men, did he intend to imply that we all have an equal share of these propensities at birth?

   ii. Consider 325c–326c. Does it appear that Protagoras regards excellence as innate or acquired?

   iii. If the civilising propensities, *dikē* and *aidōs*, are innate to a greater or lesser degree in all of us, how can Protagoras claim that the capacity for excellence can be increased by teaching?

8. Here are some possible reasons for Protagoras' rather unusual method of charging fees:
   (a) He is confident, as he says, that his students will be happy to pay, so valuable is his instruction.
   (b) He doesn't wish to be accused of gulling naïve people, and offers the second method to placate suspicious citizens.
   (c) He is concerned that all people should recognise the importance and usefulness of his instruction and

wishes to encourage people to become *kaloi k'agathoi* (328b) (cf. I.4.i).

Which does Protagoras have in mind?

    i. What impression of Protagoras is Plato trying to give his reader?

9. In his first reply to Socrates, Protagoras denied that he used any disguise for his profession of sophistry. What devices does he use to enable himself to follow his profession safely and successfully?

    i. Has he said anything which might antagonise conventional opinions on any subject?

    ii. In what ways has he adapted both style and content of this speech to suit the audience?

    iii. Assuming that Protagoras honestly believes in the merits of his profession, is he justified in using all the techniques at his disposal to present the best possible case for himself?

10. Socrates encouraged Protagoras to make this speech. He gave him an opening by his rather off-hand argument about the attitude of the Athenian assembly towards citycraft. Protagoras has now replied to these arguments. Will Socrates now, in turn, present counter-arguments on these same topics?

    i. Did Socrates intend simply to get Protagoras' opinion of the issues thus far raised?

    ii. What general qualities of Protagoras' personality, techniques and thought have emerged from this speech?

    iii. On what issues might Socrates launch an attack?

Commentary
Section XIII (328d–330b)

1. What are the advantages and disadvantages of making a speech or writing an essay, as opposed to discussing a problem using question and answer – dialogue – as a way of explaining an idea or getting at the truth about a topic?

    i. When Socrates says that he was spellbound by Protagoras' eloquence, is he being sincere or ironic?

    ii. Why does dialogue suit Socrates' purposes more than making long speeches?

2. Is Socrates genuinely being held back by a doubt about whether justice, moderation and holiness are the same, or different parts of the same excellence, or is he merely trying to pick a hole in Protagoras' argument?

    i. The concept of political excellence (*politikē aretē*) has developed in the course of the dialogue. In what sense of the term did (a) Hippocrates seek to acquire it, (b) Socrates wish to be shown that it could be taught and (c) Protagoras in his speech claim that it could be taught and that he could teach it?

    ii. Will Protagoras' answer to this question make any difference to his claim that excellence can be taught? Is Socrates being fair in not responding directly to what Protagoras said?

    iii. Which way of argument is fairer: to attack what a person says or to attack his unstated presuppositions? Under what conditions is the latter more effective than the former?

3. Socrates always begins a critical refutation (*elenchos*) of his interlocutor's views by eliciting from him a precise and unambiguous statement of his position. Thus, Socrates asks Protagoras to choose between two interpret-

102

ations of his own repeated claim that justice, moderation and holiness amount to a single thing – excellence:

(a) They amount to a single thing in the sense that they are all separate things which, taken together, compose excellence. In the same way an atom of carbon and an atom of oxygen amount to a molecule of carbon monoxide.

(b) They amount to a single thing in the sense that they are merely different words for the same quality – excellence.

Protagoras takes (a) as obviously correct. Is it obviously correct?

   i. Does it follow from (a) that no man could be said to have political excellence unless he had all three – justice, moderation and holiness? Are good men only those in whom all virtues are combined?

  ii. What arguments might one offer for (b)?

 iii. What seems to be wrong with saying of a sufferer from vertigo who rescues a child from a tenth-story ledge, that what he does is *just*; or of a landlord who has not raised the rent of a tenant who has improved the value of the property, that what he does is *courageous*?

 iv. Presumably, given your answer to (iii), you would be happier to say that what the vertigo sufferer did was not just, and that what the landlord did was not courageous – or would you?

4. Socrates tries to narrow down Protagoras' statement by offering him alternative versions of (a). Why does the first analogy, with parts of the face, seem intuitively more plausible than the second, with parts of gold?

5. Just as Socrates pinned down Hippocrates to a series of increasingly specific statements, so now he does the same to Protagoras in relation to the excellences. Is he giving what seem to be obvious replies, or is he giving considered judgments? If the latter, is there room to

Commentary

claim that any kind of expert knowledge has been involved in making the judgments?

    i. When Socrates asks whether it is possible to have one excellence without having all three, why does Protagoras find it necessary to introduce two further excellences – courage and wisdom – in order to make his point? Given that Protagoras is defending the proposition that the excellences are quite distinct, why did he not merely say that many men can be moderate without being just, or just without being holy?

    ii. What is the difference between saying that no excellence is the same kind of thing as any other *in itself* and saying that no excellence is the same kind of thing as any other *in its capacity*?

    iii. We might say that the eye is *in itself* a perceptual organ with the *capacity* of perceiving, or that it is *in itself* an optical organ with the *capacity* of seeing. Similarly we could say that the ear is *in itself* a perceptual organ with the *capacity* of perceiving, or that it is *in itself* an auditory organ with the *capacity* of hearing. If in the case of each organ we concentrated on the former description, would we have shown that they are the same kind of thing? If we concentrated on the latter description, how would we describe justice and holiness so that they were shown to be distinct kinds of things in an analogous way?

    iv. If you were Protagoras, what would you ask Socrates before answering his questions?

6. In adding courage and wisdom to justice, moderation and holiness to make five components of excellence, Protagoras is following Greek convention. Socrates, Protagoras and their audience would all agree that these terms cover the full range of virtuous attitudes and behaviour. Is the list exhaustive, or is there some other virtue which does not fall under one of these five?

Section XIV

7. Given the answers which Protagoras has provided to Socrates' questions, how will Socrates set about refuting his claim that the *aretai* are quite distinct?

   i. If it could be shown that the eye were also an auditory organ and the ear were also an optical organ, would it follow that eyes and ears are the same? Would it follow that the eye is a kind of ear?

   ii. If it could be shown that no man could be just without being moderate, or moderate without being just, would that prove that justice and moderation were the same kind of excellence with the same capacity?

Section XIV: (330b–332a)

1. At 330a–b Protagoras has committed himself to defending the claim that no one of the five excellences is the same kind of thing as any other either *in itself* or *in its capacity*. Is Protagoras' position reasonable?

   i. Is there an example of an action which is just (*dikaion*) but not wise (*sophon*), or wise but not just?

   ii. If a politician were faced with two possible courses of action, one of which he considered to be wise but not just, the other just but not wise, how would he decide which was the proper course to take?

   iii. Would you be willing to entertain the possibility that Hitler was a wise (in the sense of *sophos* – see II.5.iii) and courageous (although unjust and unholy) politician?

2. Socrates' *elenchos* (see XIII.3) proceeds by obtaining Protagoras' assent to a series of assumptions:

105

Commentary

A. Justice is some thing, not no thing. (Similarly holiness.)

B. Justice itself is a thing. (Similarly holiness.)

C. Justice itself is a just kind of thing. (Correspondingly, holiness itself is a holy kind of thing.)

D. No one excellence is the same kind of thing as any other.

Then without consulting Protagoras, he deduces from (*C*) and (*D*) that:

E. Holiness is not a just kind of thing. (Conversely justice – that is, justice is not a holy kind of thing.)

F. Holiness is an unjust kind of thing. (Conversely justice.)

But, protests Socrates:

G. Holiness is just. (Conversely justice.)

Is this a fair summary of 330c–331b, or are there hidden assumptions not stated here?

   i. Are assumptions *A*, *B*, *C* and *D* sound?

  ii. Assuming that they are sound, does *E* follow validly from *A–D*?

 iii. Does *F* follow validly from *E*?

 iv. Is Socrates logically entitled to conclude that holiness is just (*G*) and that therefore holiness and justice are the same?

NOTE: Questions 3–7 are intended to assist you in answering question 2 rather than to provide an extensive analysis of the argument (for which see C. C. W. Taylor). Letters *A–G* will throughout refer to the assumptions and conclusions of question 2. As the argument is difficult to follow, it may be useful to answer the questions in writing.

3. Consider assumptions *A* and *B*. Are they true?

   i. Is 'no thing' a plausible answer to the question 'Is justice some thing or no thing?'

106

Section XIV

ii. Why, if Protagoras had answered that justice (and holiness) is no thing, could Socrates not proceed as he does?

iii. Given the terms in which Protagoras discussed justice in his long speech, he can hardly deny that justice is something. But is there a sense in which it is possible to argue that although justice exists in the abstract, it is not a 'thing'?

iv. When we say that 'tennis balls are round and fuzzy' we are referring to the properties of a class of concrete things. But when we say that 'courage is admirable' we do not seem to be referring to a class of things in the same way. Which of these two statements does 'justice is desirable' more closely resemble?

v. Once Protagoras has accepted *A*, is he in a position to deny *B*?

vi. Could *C* be true even if *A* or *B* were false? Are *A* and *B* necessary to the argument?

4. Consider assumption *C*. Is justice a just (as opposed to unjust) kind of thing?

i. Does it seem plausible to say that justice is unjust (or that holiness is unholy)?

ii. We can object to statements like 'blackness is black' on the grounds that blackness is an attribute and as such cannot literally be black (or, indeed, have any other physical attribute). On the same ground (self-predication), it has been argued that justice (or holiness) cannot have the attribute of being just (or holy). On the other hand, whereas in the case of blackness we cannot say that it has any *physical* attributes, it seems quite proper to say of justice that it has the *moral* attributes of being good, wise or holy. Why, therefore, would it not also be proper to call it just?

Moreover, in Greek the abstract notion of justice

107

can be represented either by the noun *dikaiosunē* or by the phrase *to dikaion* (the just thing). Thus it would be natural for Protagoras and Socrates to think that 'the just thing' is just. Nevertheless, it might now be said that it was improper to speak of 'justness' (the *attribute* of being just) as being itself just. What is just is justice (i.e. the *practice* of acting justly).

Is it fair of Socrates to suggest that justice could only be just or unjust?

5. If justice is a just kind of thing (*C*) and no one excellence is the same kind of thing as any other (*D*), does it validly follow that holiness is not a just kind of thing (*E*)?

   i. Consider this argument in comparison with an argument about parts of the face, an analogy previously used by Socrates:

C. Justice is a just kind of thing.	*C*$_1$. The eye is a seeing kind of thing.
d. Holiness is not the same kind of thing as justice. (*A* specific example of the general statement *D*).	*d*$_1$. The ear is not the same kind of thing as the eye. (A specific example of the general statement about the dissimilarity of parts of the face.)
E. Holiness is not a just kind of thing.	*E*$_1$. The ear is not a seeing kind of thing.

   Is *C*$_1$–*d*$_1$ analoguous to *C*–*D*? Are *E* and *E*$_1$ valid deductions from the premise? (That is, do the conclusions seem to follow inevitably from the premises?)

   ii. Consider this pair of arguments:

C$_2$. The mammal is an air-breathing kind of thing.	*C*$_3$. The mammal is a kind of thing which is suckled at birth.

d_2. The reptile is not the same kind of thing as the mammal.

d_3. The reptile is not the same kind of thing as the mammal.

E_2. The reptile is not an air-breathing kind of thing.

E_3. The reptile is not a kind of thing which is suckled at birth.

These two arguments have the same apparent form, but in C_2–E_2 the premises seem true and the conclusion false, whereas in C_3–E_3 both premises and conclusion seem true. If either argument were valid it could not have true premises and a false conclusion, for 'valid argument' means, in part, that true premises entail a true conclusion. So what can you conclude? Is neither argument valid? Is one of the premises false? Or are these arguments not, in fact, of the same form?

NOTE: If you are not convinced by an argument that seems formally valid, it may be that some words or expressions are being used ambiguously or inconsistently.

6. Is the expression 'kind of thing' used clearly and consistently throughout these examples?

   i. Consider C_2 and C_3. We could substitute for C_3 the sentence 'The mammal is *the* kind of animal which is suckled at birth'. For being suckled at birth is *the* distinguishing, indeed, the *defining* characteristic of mammals, whereas being air-breathing is an inherent but not unique characteristic. If 'the' is substituted in C_2, that premise becomes false, whereas previously it was apparently true. How would you now answer 5.ii?

   ii. Can 'the' be substituted in C to produce a more obviously valid argument? That is, is justice, and only justice (not holiness or any other excellence), *the* just kind of thing?

   iii. If you say that justice, and only justice, is *the* just

109

kind of thing, does it follow that no other excellence can be just (see 6.i)? Or, if you say that justice cannot be *the* only just kind of thing (and hence, that we cannot legitimately substitute 'the' in *C*), is the term 'just' of no more special relevance to justice than to any other excellence?

iv. In which way – as a statement of an inherent attribute or as a defining characteristic – must 'kind of thing' be understood if Socrates' conclusion *E* is to follow validly from *C* and *D*?

v. When Protagoras claimed that no two excellences were the same kind of thing, did he mean that no two excellences can have the same defining characteristics, or that no two excellences can have any attribute whatsoever in common?

vi. Reconsider XIII.5.iii, where the same distinction between inherent and defining characteristics was alluded to. We see not merely because we have various organs with the capacity of perceiving, but because we have eyes, which are organs with the capacity of seeing (as opposed to the ears, perceptual organs with the capacity of hearing). Are men just in virtue of their possessing excellence in general, or because they have some specific capacity for acting justly (as opposed to, say, piously or courageously)?

vii. There clearly is a shift in meaning of the expression 'kind of thing' which affects the validity of Socrates' argument in some way, although it is difficult to state precisely how. Given that a Greek might perceive no difference between saying that 'justice is *a* just kind of thing (*dikaion*)' and 'justice *the* just kind of thing (*to dikaion*) – cf. 4.ii – how does the possibility that neither Socrates nor Protagoras (nor indeed Plato) is aware of this ambiguity affect your interpretation and criticism of this argument?

Section XIV

7. Consider conclusion *F*. Would it follow from the fact that justice is not a holy kind of thing (or that holiness is not a just kind of thing), that justice is an unholy kind of thing (or that holiness is an unjust kind of thing)?

    i. Are all acts necessarily either just or unjust, holy or unholy? Are there examples of actions which are neither?

    ii. Apparently some actions have nothing to do with justice or holiness. But if a man in the street were asked whether it is right or wrong to do what is not just, how would he reply, and why?

    iii. If justice is not holy, can any just act *qua* just (that is, insofar as it is just) be holy? If all acts which are just are holy *because* they are just, can there be a definition of justice which does not include the whole class of holy things (and conversely for holiness)?

    iv. What is the difference between justice and holiness? Do they denote distinct kinds of goodness in the same way that red and green denote different (and mutually exclusive) kinds of colour? Or do they represent different points of view from which we express our approval of the same unitary goodness?

8. Consider these three comments on Socrates' argument:
    (a) Socrates (or Plato) is cheating (or is muddled). His argument rests on ambiguities of everyday speech. It can therefore be dismissed.
    (b) Whether or not Socrates (or Plato) is explicitly aware of the ambiguities of his questions, the argument reveals an inconsistency in the way we use value-language. Thus while we take justice and holiness as quite distinct virtues, yet it seems paradoxical to say that something could be just without also being holy, and *vice versa*.

Commentary

    (c)   The validity of Socrates' argument is less important than what he is doing to Protagoras.
To what extent are any or all of these true?

9. We have already noted Protagoras' anxiety to conciliate public opinion. How has Socrates exploited that fact to ensnare him?

    i.   Why, in this passage, does Socrates first ask Protagoras about assumptions *A* and *B* directly and then continue by pretending that some member of the general public is asking the questions of both Socrates and Protagoras?

    ii.   Socrates says that justice is just, but asks Protagoras 'Which way would you vote?' Again, instead of saying simply that holiness is holy, he puts on a show of outrage, suggesting that the contrary position is blasphemous. What effect do these additions have on Protagoras' attitude to the questions? Does he think that he is being asked to classify holiness as a just kind of thing, or to make a value-judgment about holiness? What prevents him from saying that holiness is not holy?

    iii.   Next, Socrates dissociates himself from Protagoras' claim (*D*). What is his motive? What is Plato's dramatic purpose?

    iv.   Why does Socrates himself introduce *E*, *F*, *G* and the conclusion that justice and holiness are the same thing, without giving Protagoras the opportunity to answer each point?

    v.   How is Protagoras likely to react when he discovers that he is suddenly committed to the view that holiness is unjust and justice unholy?

10. We have seen that much of Socrates' *elenchos* is questionable, particularly because many of his questions are open to more than one interpretation. Does Protagoras, in his final response, show a clear understanding of why

112

Section XIV

Socrates has been able to use assumptions *A*, *B* and *C* to create a contradiction between *D* and *G*?

   i. Is the tone of Protagoras' attempt to get out of the apparent contradiction (331d–e) confident?

  ii. Could Socrates' argument in fact, as Protagoras claims, be used to prove that black is the same as white?

 iii. Why, in the end, is Protagoras willing to concede assumption *G*?

 iv. Bearing in mind Socrates' true motive for talking to Protagoras, why does he reject Protagoras' concession, made for the sake of argument, and insist on an examination of 'me and you'.

  v. Does Protagoras sound, at the end, as though he thinks he got the better of the argument?

11. This Section is intended to raise problems rather than to solve them. Nevertheless, here are some conclusions which might be drawn. Are they all justified? Which might be drawn by Protagoras? By Socrates? By Hippocrates? By the audience at Callias' house? By Plato?

  (a) Assumptions which both Socrates and Protagoras find unobjectionable may be questionable, indeed, untenable.

  (b) Socrates is fully aware of the ambiguities inherent in the assumptions on which he builds his argument, but Protagoras is not.

  (c) If the assumptions are untenable, then Protagoras' position, that the *aretai* are quite distinct, is proved.

  (d) Socrates has proved that at least two *aretai* are either the same or more closely related than Protagoras has assumed.

  (e) Socrates has caught Protagoras with a verbal trick: if something is not holy, then it must be unholy.

  (f) Protagoras has not been refuted if we agree that,

Commentary

while being just may be an attribute of holiness, that does not make holiness a kind of justice in the required sense.

(g) Value-words cannot strictly speaking have value-attributes in the same way that concrete things can have concrete attributes.

(h) Plato intends to raise in our minds a doubt about how clear we are about what we mean by our everyday moral judgments.

(i) Protagoras is in danger of affronting conventional morality if he continues to maintain that the *aretai* are completely different.

(j) Protagoras and Socrates have different reasons for holding this kind of investigation.

(k) Protagoras is easily flustered.

(l) Socrates is a bit of a sophist; his arguments look superficially plausible until you examine their meaning.

(m) Protagoras, if he is an expert, ought not to have been caught by this argument. Therefore he cannot justify his claim to teach the excellences, since he does not understand how they are related and, by extension, cannot understand of what they consist.

i Is it possible for a text to embody problem and consequences which the author did not himself see or understand? Or would it be belittling Plato to suggest that he did not see the implications of what he wrote?

Section XV (332a–333b)

1. Socrates continues his *elenchos* by asking whether folly (*aphrosunē*) is the absolute opposite of wisdom (*sophia*). Is he, in effect, asking whether anyone who is not a fool must be wise, and *vice versa* (i.e. whether folly and

114

wisdom are contradictories), or whether wisdom is at the opposite end of the scale from folly, with mediocre qualities like 'good sense' between the extremes (i.e. whether they are polar opposites)?

  i. Would either Socrates or Protagoras have thought so precisely about the meaning of the question?

2. Socrates next asks whether those who act rightly (*orthōs*) and advantageously (*ophelimōs*) are controlling their actions (*sōphronein*). This statement could be taken in two ways. An action can be performed *orthōs* either in the sense that it was executed without mistakes and brought to a successful conclusion, or in the sense that it was the right thing to do. Hence to do something rightly and advantageously could mean either to do it successfully and beneficially (to oneself), or to do what is right and beneficial (in relation to others). Similarly *sōphrosunē* can denote the ability to control one's actions either in the sense of having the intelligence to choose sensible goals and accomplish them, or in the sense of exercising moderation or self-restraint (in relation to the law and to one's fellow citizens). Which sense does Protagoras use in his answer to Socrates?

  i. Look, in Protagoras' long speech, at the uses of the word *sōphrosunē* at 323a, 323b, 325a and 326a. Which uses denote the moral and which the practical *aretē*?

  ii. In which of the two senses is *sōphrosunē* a political excellence?

  iii. Given that it has just been established that folly (*aphrosunē*) is the opposite of wisdom (*sophia*), in which of the two senses is acting foolishly (*aphronōs*) the opposite of acting in a self-controlled manner (*sōphronōs*)?

3. Is it true that a given attribute can have only one attribute as its opposite?

Commentary

i. In which of the two senses of 'opposite' discussed in (1) is 'inaccurate' the opposite of 'accurate'?

ii. 'Sweet' can have as its opposites 'sour', 'bitter' or 'savoury'. In what sense of 'opposite' does 'sweet' have these three distinct opposites?

4. Is Socrates now right to conclude that since both *sophia* and *sōphrosunē* are opposites of *aphrosunē* they must constitute one and the same *aretē*?

i. Are they both opposites of *aphrosunē* in the same sense, or is *sophia* its extreme opposite, while *sōphrosunē* is the mean between the two?

ii. Does the sense of *sōphrosunē* (see 2), in which it is an opposite of *aphrosunē*, at least make it closely related to *sophia*?

iii. We have already seen two distinct ways in which a man can be said to control his action and hence be *sōphrōn*. In the sense in which *sophia* denotes an *aretē* related to citycraft, can a man be said to be *sophos* who does not restrain impulses to personal excess and wrongdoing on the one hand, and yet who is able to find effective means for accomplishing desired ends on the other?

iv. What is the difference between (a) a wise statesman and a clever statesman and (b) a prudent statesman and a cautious statesman?

v. Must a man who is *sophrōn* also be *sophos*? If not, what additional quality does he need?

5. Is Socrates' argument fair?

i. We have seen that Socrates' questions appear deceptively simple. Is it fair to test Protagoras' professed expertise by laying traps for him?

ii. After getting Protagoras to agree that acting in a self-controlled manner (*sōphronōs*) is the opposite of acting foolishly (*aphronōs*), Socrates

116

uses a lengthy argument to prove that self-control (*sōphrosunē*) is therefore the opposite of folly (*aphrosunē*) (interrupting this argument with the further proof that nothing can have more than one opposite). Is an argument of such length necessary? Does it make it easier or more difficult for Protagoras to follow the direction of the argument?

iii. If the argument is flawed, why does Plato make Protagoras accept its conclusion without demur?

iv. How would we decide whether Socrates (or Plato) is aware of the complexities of his questions, or whether he merely has an instinct for tough questions?

v. Would Socrates have been any more successful at answering his own questions? If he had not been, would he have found this failure embarrassing?

6. In refuting Protagoras, Socrates has argued that *dikaiosunē* and *hosiotēs* are virtually the same *aretē*, while *sophia* and *sōphrosunē* are actually identical. If A=B and C=D, what must be done to show that A=B=C=D?

Section XVI (333b–335c)

1. Give an example in which it would be true to say that it would be sound (*sōphronein*) for a man to commit an injustice (*adikein*).

2. In Protagoras' speech *sōphrosunē* was translated as 'moderation'; for the preceding section 'self-control' was more suitable. In this case the word 'soundness' more accurately captures the dilemma with which Protagoras is faced: in what sense of *sōphrosunē* would it be

117

shameful to Protagoras to agree that injustice could be a *sōphron* thing to commit (cf. XI.7; XV.2)?

3. Why does Socrates not mind whether they discuss Protagoras' own view or the popular view?

    i. Had Protagoras chosen a discussion of his own view, how might Socrates have attacked him?

    ii. Why does Protagoras choose to examine the popular view?

4. Socrates says that 'Protagoras tried to make excuses, and claimed that it was a complicated question'. Why is Protagoras unwilling to defend the opinion of the many 'whether the view is your own or not'?

    i. Why might someone be unwilling to defend a view which is not his own?

    ii. Protagoras himself chose the view to be examined. Why has he suddenly changed his mind?

5. Protagoras has admitted that to say that it can be sound (*sōphronein*) for a man to commit an injustice (*adikein*) is equivalent to the claim that it can be good sense (*eu phronein*) to do so. This in turn, Protagoras agrees, is true in the sense that a man can be exercising good planning (*eu bouleuesthai*) in committing an injustice (*adikein*), if he does well (*eu prattein*) by it. At 318e he claimed to teach *euboulia*. Why might he be unhappy with the direction of this argument?

    i. We have seen that there are two sides to *euboulia* and to the excellence of citycraft (cf. VII; VIII): one is the ability to be a political success; the other is the ability to be a good citizen. We have also seen that Protagoras is anxious to play down the former and to stress the latter aspect. Why might he find this restatement of the popular view embarrassing?

    ii. Could Protagoras then deny that if his course of

instruction involves the teaching of *sōphrosunē*, then since *sōphrosunē* can enable men to succeed by means of injustice his course must also give men this ability?

iii. Would the fact that he is merely expressing the view of the many exonerate him from this charge?

6. Socrates next establishes that there are good things (*agatha*) which are beneficial (*ōphelima*). Why does Protagoras break into the argument here?

   i. Consider Protagoras' presentation of the conventional view of *dikaiosunē* and *sōphrosunē* in the long speech (322e–323c). Would Protagoras be able to agree that, in the popular view, injustice (*adikia*) can be a good thing (*agathon*) to do (i.e. beneficial to men) if one can succeed (*eu prattein*) by means of it?

   ii. *Eu* (well) serves as the adverb of *agathos* (good). Thus it might be said that, if someone does well (*eu prattein*) in performing some action, that action was a good thing (*agathon*) to do (see XXI.2.vii). How would this substitution help Socrates refute the popular view?

   iii. Would Socrates have thus succeeded in showing that the popular view was mistaken, or that Protagoras' claim that it was the popular view was mistaken?

   iv. Given the ambiguity of 'being a good thing (*agathon*) to do' (i.e. a morally right thing or a personally beneficial thing), would such a refutation have been fair?

7. Protagoras argues that the goodness or benefit of a thing can only be assessed in relation to specific cases. Do you agree?

   i. If you do not agree, can you think of anything which is good, but not good for some specific thing?

Commentary

ii. If you agree, would you therefore say that nothing (not even justice) can be good in and of itself? Could there, for example, be any conceivable circumstance under which being healthy would not be good or beneficial?

iii. Would being healthy be a good state for Hitler to be in – or for a rat? Good for whom?

iv. Does Protagoras' response constitute a refutation of Socrates' line of argument? Why does the audience respond so enthusiastically?

8. Is Socrates justified in demanding that Protagoras argue according to Socrates' method of question and answer, rather than use the tech...que of presenting a case in a long speech – a technique in which Protagoras is clearly expert?

i. Are we meant to sympathise with Socrates' complaint that he cannot hold ideas in his head, or is he just being petulant?

ii. Was it any easier to follow the thread of Socrates' argument in Section XV (cf. XV.5.ii) than this mini-speech of Protagoras?

iii. If Protagoras insists on using a style of debate in which Socrates claims to be incompetent, and then wins, will his victory be a fair one?

iv. Does Protagoras' remark at 335a suggest that he is concerned to solve Socrates' difficulty (cf. 329e), or that he is treating the discussion as a contest?

v. Suppose we were discussing a problem with someone who is an expert in a field – for instance, discussing with a nuclear physicist the merits of building nuclear reactors for generating electricity – would we be justified in feeling annoyed if the physicist dominated the conversation?

vi. On what is Protagoras an expert?

Section XVII

9. We have seen that this dialogue is a work of philosophy, a polemical attack on sophistic training and a dramatic narrative. How are these three purposes reflected in the three arguments presented by Socrates (cf. XIV, XV, XVI)?

   i. Given that all these arguments have been inconclusive or logically dubious, is Plato concerned primarily to prove that the *aretai* are identical, or to raise questions about whether we have a sufficiently clear understanding of our everyday moral judgments or of the language we use to make them?

   ii. The last argument was left unfinished. Thus we are left with the unrefuted claim that injustice can be a sound and sensible way of achieving one's ends, provided one can get away with it. Is it likely that Plato will leave such a claim in the air?

   iii. How is this unrefuted claim relevant to Socrates' original purpose of assessing whether sophistic training in general and Protagoras' course of instruction in particular are beneficial or harmful to the mind?

   iv. In what ways have the foregoing arguments assisted Socrates in this original purpose?

   v. In what ways has Plato developed the characters of Socrates and Protagoras in the course of these arguments?

   vi. With what dramatic purpose does Plato break off the third argument without completing it? What does the reader expet to happen next?

Section XVII (335c–338e)

1. Is this interlude of general discussion among Callias'

121

Commentary

guests necessary for the development of the philosophical topics raised by Socrates and Hippocrates, and by Socrates and Protagoras?

    i. If there are ideas here relevant to the previous debate, why did Plato not continue the direct confrontation between Socrates and Protagoras? Wouldn't that have been a more efficient way to pursue the issues already raised?

    ii. If this interlude seems irrelevant to the philosophical debate, why did Plato include it?

    iii. What themes other than philosophical ones are being developed in this dialogue?

2. In the dialogue so far we have identified several strands: (a) a philosophical inquiry; (b) a portrayal of Socrates; (c) a dramatic narrative; (d) an attack on the sophists and their educational claims. What does this section contribute to each of these?

    i. Re-read 314e–317e. What similarities are there between the two scenes?

    ii. In what respects are the minor characters developed in this scene?

    iii. How does the relationship between the two main characters differ in the two scenes?

3. Socrates often uses *eironeia*, mock-modesty, in the form of either exaggerated self-depreciation or exaggerated praise of others. For what purposes has Socrates used *eironeia* in the past (consider 319a–b; 320b; 328d–e; 334c–d)? For what purpose does he use it here?

    i. Socrates uses the metaphor of a foot-race to describe the discourse Protagoras and he have been conducting. How does this metaphorical picture compare with his own view of discourse?

4. Is Critias right to accuse Callias and Alcibiades of taking sides in what he hints has become a contest?

Section XVII

i. Why does Alcibiades think that Callias' solution favours Protagoras?

ii. If each speaks as he sees fit, as Callias proposes, is their discussion likely to get anywhere?

iii. Considering what Socrates thinks is the purpose of a discussion, is Alcibiades right to say 'If, therefore, Protagoras in turn admits that he is inferior to Socrates in debate, Socrates is content'?

5. At 315e Socrates called Prodicus a wise man, and at 341a he will mention that he has studied with Prodicus. Does the tone and content of this speech suggest that it is a portrait by an admiring student?

   i. What is the difference between Socrates' interest in asking what things are and Prodicus' interest in precise semantic distinctions?

   ii. Given that Hippocrates wants to become a clever speaker in popular assemblies (see IV.5.i) and law courts (see IV.6.i), in which of these fields would Prodicus' technique be more useful to him?

   iii. What solution is Prodicus proposing for the practical problem of how to go on with the discussion?

   iv. What is Plato satirising in Prodicus' speech?

6. What is Plato satirising in Hippias' speech?

   i. Satire generally involves the exaggeration of the salient features of the object of the satire. What features of Hippias' style of oratory are being sent up here?

   ii. See 5.ii. In which of these fields – political or forensic oratory – would Hippias' technique be more useful to Hippocrates?

   iii. The distinction between nature (*phusis*) and law or convention (*nomos*) assumed widespread importance in the thinking of late fifth-century Greece. The sophist Antiphon (see XI.5.i) main-

123

tained that justice amounts to a set of artificial
conventions imposed upon man in violation of nature, and with no true basis in reality. According
to Antiphon, there is nothing wrong with break-
ing the law, provided you are not caught. If, he
thought, there is any reason why one man should
not harm another, it must derive from the existence of a natural affinity among human beings. In
Plato's *Gorgias* the young sophist-trained orator
Callicles goes further. According to him conventional justice is humbug. According to natural justice, the stronger are by nature better and
therefore have the right to dominate and exploit
the weaker by any means in their power. The view
that it is *sōphron* to commit *adikia* could be interpreted in terms of this distinction. According to
Socrates it could never be (by convention) *sōphron* to commit *adikia*. But the general opinion is
that it could be (by nature) *sōphron* – that is,
sound policy in one's own interest – to do so. The
opposed points of view would thus be at cross purposes (see XVI.1–2; 5). What does Hippias mean,
then, when he calls *nomos* the 'tyrant of
humanity'?

iv. If Hippias' proposal were accepted and a referee
chosen, would that end the purely competitive nature of the debate and turn it into a discussion
among brother-sophists, as Hippias wants?

7. Is Socrates' response to Hippias' proposal a sophistical
argument or a sincere attempt at a workable compromise?

i. If this speech seems sincere, does Socrates really
think that no one is wiser than Protagoras?

ii. If this speech seems ironic and sophistical, why
should Plato suddenly undermine the characterisation of Socrates as an honest seeker after the
truth on behalf of Hippocrates?

Section XVIII

8. Why is Protagoras unwilling to continue?

   i. Who has won the argument about debating method?

   ii. Is the rest of the dialogue likely to consist of short question-and-answer?

Section XVIII (338e–342c)

1. The dialogue between Socrates and Protagoras is resumed in this section, after an interval during which the conversation nearly disintegrated. How does the tone and content of their exchange in this section differ from the earlier arguments about *dikaiosunē*, *sōphrosunē*, *hosiotēs* and *sophia*?

2. Protagoras presents this argument as a sample of his teaching methods. What would a student learn from having his assumptions refuted in this way?

   i. Compare Protagoras' *elenchos* in this passage with the arguments used by Socrates against Hippocrates at 311b–314c. What did Hippocrates learn from being subjected to Socrates' cross-questioning (V.1.i)? What, on the other hand, would he learn from submitting to Protagoras' cross-questioning?

   ii. How would the kind of teaching of which Protagoras has just given a sample at 338e–339e help a pupil to become a clever speaker?

3. Here is the full text of Simonides poem in English:*

---

* *We are following the reconstruction of the text in D. L. Page, Poeti Melici Graeci* (Oxford, 1962), Fr. 542. The poem is of four stanzas, each ten lines in length. Thus lines 4–10 are missing. Passages in angled brackets are doubtful. Probably they are paraphrases by Socrates, more or less accurate, of the original.

Commentary

To be (*genesthai*) a good (*agathos*) man in truth, I admit (*men*),
is hard – a man in mind and frame
a flawless minting foursquare struck. . .   3
[*Seven lines missing to complete first stanza.*]

Yet (*de*) Pittacus' familiar words, I find, do not   11
ring true, though they come from a wise man:
It is hard (*chalepon*), he said, to be (*emmenai*) noble.
A god alone can have that privilege, while a man
can not escape being (*emmenai*) bad (*kakos*)   15
dragged down by helpless circumstance.
For if he does well any man is good,
but bad if he does badly;
<While best for longest are those
whom the gods love. . .>   20

So I'll not waste my lifetime's meagre ration
on an empty dream, in search of what can never
ever be (*genesthai*): that flawless man
among us who for our living
toil in the broad earth.   25
Should I find one, I'll let you know.
I praise and love all men
who do no evil (*aischron*) willingly (*hekōn*)
Even the gods
do not combat necessity.   30

<I'm no harsh judge: good enough for me the man   33
who's not all bad> nor lawless to excess,
who knows the worth of justice, bastion of cities;   35
a sound man: I'll find no fault with him.
Without number the breed of fools.
You see, all things are noble
which bear not evil's taint.   40

What is Protagoras seeking to prove about this poem
(see 339e) and how does he set about proving it?

4. Who has the better of the argument, Protagoras or
Socrates?

   i. By what steps does Protagoras reach his (un-
stated) conclusion? Are all the assumptions true?
Is the argument valid? (Try setting out the steps
of the argument as in IX.2.i or XIV.2.)

   ii. Consider Socrates' counter-argument (340a–d).

Section XVIII

Assuming that Simonides had intended to draw a distinction between *genesthai* and *emmenai* (see footnote to 339b), how is the validity of Protagoras' argument affected? Which steps of the argument would be refuted?

iii. What is Protagoras' objection at 340d? Is it convincing?

iv. Socrates now redirects his defence. Without explicitly giving up his distinction between *genesthai* and *emmenai*, he re-enlists Prodicus in an attempt to suggest that Simonides, by *chalepon*, meant 'bad'. What is Simonides now supposed to be saying, according to Socrates and Prodicus? How does this differ from what Socrates previously claimed he was saying (see 340c–d)?

v. How does this overcome Protagoras' objection at 340e and so enable Socrates to hold on to his distinction?

vi. Considering what Simonides said in line 1, is it likely that he meant 'bad' instead of 'hard'?

vii. Should we accept (a) Protagoras', (b) Socrates' reason for denying that Simonides meant 'bad' by *chalepon*?

viii. Has Protagoras won the argument?

5. Re-read the poem as a whole. Is Protagoras' *elenchos* based on a plausible interpretation of Simonides' meaning?

i. Does Simonides appear to contradict himself in the first two stnzas?

ii. Simonides' poetry was well-known and respected among the educated. Socrates maintains that he has 'made a detailed study' of this poem to Scopas. Is it likely that it contains a major contradiction of the kind pointed out by Protagoras?

iii. If Protagoras' version is not plausible, can Simon-

ides' poem be interpreted so that it does not appear
to contradict itself?

6. Protagoras scornfully rejects Prodicus' suggestion that
   Simonides understood *chalepon* in the saying of Pittacus
   to mean 'bad', and Socrates agrees that Prodicus was
   pulling Protagoras' leg. Is Socrates right, or was Prodicus making a serious argument?

   i. From what we have seen of Prodicus (337a–c),
      what methods would you expect him to use to
      establish the meaning of a disputed passage?

   ii. Would a specialist knowledge of the dictionary
       meanings of each word used by a poet enable us
       to establish with certainty what his poem meant?
       If not, why not?

   iii. If Prodicus' point is made in jest, and manifestly
        so, why does Socrates introduce it? Why does Prod-
        icus co-operate?

7. At 339e the audience erupts into applause. Is this
   because:
   (a) Protagoras has revealed a genuine and hitherto
       unnoticed flaw in a famous poem, or
   (b) in the contest which has developed between Pro-
       tagoras and Socrates, Protagoras has made a
       clever winning move?

   i. In his description of the audience's and his own
      reaction at 339e–340a, is Socrates trying to con-
      vey to his friend an atmosphere in which the par-
      ties involved are concerned mainly with the truth
      about Simonides' meaning?

   ii. In the light of Protagoras' attitude expressed at
       335a and the course the discussion had taken up
       to that point, what does Protagoras hope to accom-
       plish from this argument?

   iii. Reconsider 6.iii. Does the behaviour of Socrates
        and Prodicus suggest that they are concerned with

Section XIX

Simonides' true meaning or with conducting a trial of wits?

8. At 342a Socrates offers to give a full interpretation of the poem. Protagoras rather grudgingly accepts, but the others, particularly Prodicus and Hippias, greet the suggestion with enthusiasm. Why?

    i. If someone had claimed detailed knowledge of something and then had been refuted in discussion about it, would you be eager to listen to him expounding that subject at length?

    ii. Before, the audience applauded Protagoras for his successful *elenchos*. Has anything happened to make them change their attitude?

Section XIX (342c–348b)

1. Socrates does not immediately begin his exegesis. Instead he launches into a lengthy discussion of the background of the saying of Pittacus and Simonides' motive for attaching it. What is Plato's reason for inserting this passage?

    i. Compare Socrates' tale about the Spartans with Protagoras' introductory story about Prometheus and Epimetheus (320c–323a). Consider each, moreover, in relation to the whole speech of which it is a part. In what respects are they similar? In what respects different?

    ii. In saying that the Spartans are renowned philosophers, Socrates is being ironic. The Spartans (of the fifth century B.C., at least) were not philosophers but a notoriously dour and uncultivated people of few words and fewer ideas. They lived in a state of perpetual military readiness, and brought up their young under a brutally tough regimen. Given that Socrates opens in this way, in what spirit is his audience likely to regard the subsequent exposition?

iii. At 342b Socrates uses Protagoras' argument that sophists conceal their true identiy, calling themselves among other things, poets (see 316sq. and VII.2). Is it likely that he is serious in suggesting that Simonides' intentions are sophistic?

iv. Protagoras had declared his intention to test Socrates' skill in the discussion of poetry. As he listens to Socrates, do you think he will feel that Socrates is proceeding in the spirit he had intended?

2. Does Socrates' interpretation of the first two stanzas, taken with the second two stanzas, provide a plausible and satisfactory explanation of the overall meaning of the poem?

i. How far does Socrates' interpretation of the first two stanzas of the poem differ from his previous interpretation at 340c ff.?

ii. Does Socrates' interpretation of Simonides' own beliefs about the possibility of goodness in the second pair of stanzas conform to their evident common-sense meaning?

iii. In presenting his exegesis which parts of the poem has Socrates actually misrepresented?

3. Are the kinds of argument which Socrates uses in support of his interpretation appropriate ways of analysing a poet's meaning?

i. An otherwise weak argument can often be made to look more convincing by the introduction of arguments based on expert rhetorical knowledge. How is this technique used at 343d–344a (see footnote to 343d, and 346d–e)?

Section XIX

ii. Does Socrates intend his audience to be able to analyse each of his arguments critically (see X.4)?

iii. In his long speech Protagoras made use of plausible generalisations from experience (see XII.i.ii; XII.2). What, by contrast, is Socrates' method of impressing his arguments upon his audience?

iv. What similarities and differences of clarity and soundness are there between these arguments and those used earlier by Socrates against Protagoras at 330b–331c?

4. Socrates says that 'willingly' (*hekōn*) must refer to 'praise and love' rather than to 'do no evil' (lines 27–8), since no wise man believes that anyone does wrong willingly, a proposition known as the 'Socratic Paradox'. *Hekōn* means willingly; but actions performed *hekōn* contrast with three distinct kinds of not-*hekōn* actions. I can do something not-*hekōn* because (a) I have been compelled to do it, or because (b) I had no reasonable alternative than to do it, or because (c) I did it by mistake. What all have in common is that I do something which I would not have chosen to do had I been free to choose. According to the Socratic Paradox, whatever we do, we do in pursuit of what we consider to be a good (*agathon*). If therefore we pursue what is in fact not a good, but a bad (*kakon*), we cannot have done so *hekōn*. Is this true?

i. If you say that it *is* true, and that men only do wrong not-*hekōn*, would it follow that men are in no way responsible for their wrong-doings?

ii. If you say that it is *not* true, why does Socrates assert so confidently that wise men would say that it *is* true?

iii. How would the man in the street respond to the suggestion that no man does wrong willingly?

iv. Socrates makes this assertion in the context of a patently sophistic speech. Why then does he assert

131

Commentary

without proof something which is so contrary to convention?

5. The trouble with talk about literature and with literary exegesis, says Socrates (cf. 347e), is that no one can disprove what anyone else says. How does his analysis of Simonides' poem illustrate this point?

   i. Whether or not Socrates has misrepresented Simonides' meaning (see 2.ii–iii), can Socrates' interpretation be conclusively disproved?

   ii. Which particular points in Socrates' exegesis do you regard as implausible or dubious?

   iii. Can you in each case *prove* Socrates wrong without appealing to vague notions of common sense?

   iv. Can there be such a thing as an interpretation which is both objective and definitive, or does a poem mean whatever anyone thinks it means?

   v. What specific conditions are there which limit the range of possible interpretations of a poem?

   vi. Protagoras teaches literary criticism as part of his course of instruction. How do the arguments with which Socrates supports his interpretation serve to highlight his attitude towards such teaching?

6. At the beginning of this part of the dialogue Protagoras said: 'My question still concerns the topic which you and I were discussing just now – excellence, that is – but transferred to the context of poetry. . .' (cf. 339a). Would Socrates agree that poetry can enlighten us about ethics?

   i. What did Protagoras think could be learned from studying poetry (see XVIII.2)?

   ii. Why does Socrates here repeat his concern for 'putting ourselves to the test of truth' (348a) (see 331c; 333c)?

Section XX

7. At 342a Protagoras sounded a bit disgruntled in telling Socrates he might proceed with his exegesis of the poem. Why, at 348b, is Protagoras reluctant to continue (see 1.iv)?

   i. With what aim did Protagoras embark on the discussion of poetry? Has he succeeded in that aim?

   ii. 'But Prodicus and Hippias and the others warmly urged me to go ahead.' (342a) Why were the other sophists and the audience so keen to hear Socrates' exegesis?

   iii. Why does Hippias now offer (347a–b) to give his own interpretation of the poem?

   iv. Considering 3 and 4 above, what are the other sophists and Callias' guests likely to think of Socrates now?

   v. How will Socrates use his chance to ask questions (see XV.6)?

Section XX (348b–351b)

1. After carefully recapitulating the argument, as is necessary after such a long interval, Socrates asks Protagoras, with some irony, whether he has changed his position at all. Protagoras grudgingly concedes that *sophia*, *sōphrosunē*, *dikaiosunē* and *hosiotēs* are 'tolerably close'. Why has he conceded the similarity of *sōphrosunē* and *dikaiosunē* (see 333b–334c and XVI.5–6)?

   i. Is he thereby recognising that Socrates' argument, insofar as we can discern where it was leading, was sound?

   ii. Or is he simply recognising that his own belief that *sōphrosunē* must be *dikaion* (336b) involves him in this qualified admission?

133

Commentary

2. Protagoras argues not only that *sophia* (wisdom; but see II.5.iii) and *andreia* are distinct, but also that *andreia* has nothing to do with the other *aretai*; even the most unjust *(adikos)*, unholy *(anhosios)*, unruly, ignorant *(amathēs)* person can be exceedingly courageous *(andreios)*. What must Socrates show about *andreia* such that, if it is true, Protagoras must be wrong?

    i. Socrates immediately asks Protagoras if he calls the courageous *tharraleoi*. The verb *tharrein* means to be of good heart, and a man is of good heart *(tharrei)* when he does something generally agreed to be dangerous (or which 'many men fear to face', as Protagoras puts it), whether because he is not deterred by the danger, or because he is confident of the outcome. Thus *tharraleos* can mean either (a) confident, unafraid, or (b) daring, willing to face danger. Its abstract noun is *tharros* (confidence, daring, good cheer). Does Protagoras mean to classify the *andreioi* as confident, daring, or both?

   ii. If *andreia* is simply readiness to meet what many men fear to face, in virtue of what would it be one of the *aretai*? What is it, in other words, that makes courage a quality which would be recognised as desirable for a rational man to have?

  iii. Could we admire courage if its effects were genuinely harmful, or respect a prodigiously stupid man for his courage?

  iv. Could we respect a villain for his courage?

3. Socrates' argument proceeds thus:
   (Note: Remember that *epistēmē* and *sophia* are being used interchangeably (see II.5.iii)
   Assumption A: The *andreioi* are *tharraleoi* (See 2.1).
   Assumption B: All *aretē* and so all *andreia* must be *kalon*.
   Assumption C: Tharros is produced by *epistēmē*.

Section XX

Assumption D: *Tharros* can also be produced by ignorance (*amathia*).

Conclusion E: *Tharros*, the kind involved in *andreia*, must be the effect of *epistēmē* (since to be *tharraleos* because of *amathia* cannot be *andreia* – from *B* – since it is not *kalon*, not, that is, a desirable quality for a rational man to have).

Has Socrates proved *E*?

i. See 2.i–ii. How does the way *tharraleos* and *tharros* are understood affect the validity of the argument?

ii. Is the diving expert any more *andreios* than the foolhardy men of *D*?

iii. The apparent soundness of the argument rests on the fact that *C* and *D* are proved by examples in which *tharraleos* has the connotation of 'confident', which is unrelated to 'daring' in any sense relevant to *andreia* (*Assumption A*). Why, nevertheless, might the argument have seemed plausible to Socrates and Protagoras?

4. In the light of 2 above, and given his admission of *B*, can Protagoras any longer deny that *epistēmē* is somehow involved in *andreia*?

i. If Protagoras admits that a man who, doing out of ignorance what others fear, cannot be *andreios*, can he maintain that someone can be utterly ignorant and yet be exceedingly *andreios*?

ii. Does Socrates point out this consequence of the argument?

5. Socrates' argument concludes thus:
Assumption F: The wise are *tharraleoi*.
Assumption G: The *tharraleoi* are *andreioi*

Commentary

Conclusion H: Sophia is (the same as) *andreia.*

Assuming that *E* is true, has Socrates proved *H*?

i. If *andreia* must always involve *epistēmē* (*E*) and
    if *sophia/epistēmē* are present in the courageous
    (*F* and *G*) is *sophia* the same as *andreia*?

ii. Compare the sense of *tharraleos* being employed
    in *A* and *F* (see 3.iii). Is it legitimate to deduce
    from these two assumptions (a) that all the know-
    ledgeable are *tharraleoi* (i.e. confident), and (b) all
    tharraleoi (i.e. daring) are courageous, that there-
    fore all the knowledgeable are courageous?

iii. Consider *G*. Protagoras isn't asked if he accepts it;
     but can Socrates claim to have shown that the
     tharraleoi are courageous?

iv. Protagoras agreed to Socrates' question: 'Then
    what about the courageous? Didn't you call them
    the tharraleoi?' Is this offering a definition or a
    description of the courageous (see XIV.6.i–iii)?

v. If Socrates is asking whether the courageous are
    tharraleoi and the *tharraleoi* courageous (i.e. ask-
    ing for a definition of the courageous), how does
    this affect the validity of *H*? If, on the other hand,
    he is only asking whether the courageous are *thar-
    raleoi*, why does he ask whether the courageous
    are *the tharraleoi*?

vi. All things considered, is *H* validly deduced?

6. If the argument were sound, what would Socrates have
   proved?

i. We have seen that *sophia* includes at least two
    things: the knowledge of means (i.e. expertise,
    know-how); and the broader understanding of
    ends – the ability to form rational long-term plans
    (what *we* might call wisdom). Earlier (319b–d)
    Socrates argued that *aretē* could not be taught
    because it was not a technical skill. In our present

136

passage, Socrates has unsuccessfully tried to show that *andreia* is *sophia* in the sense that a man is *andreios* in a particular action if and only if he exercises some specific expertise (*epistēmē* or *technē*) in performing it (see II.5.iii). If the argument were sound, would Socrates have shown that *andreia* was itself a separate expertise?

ii. If so, in what specific field does a man have to have *epistēmē* in order to be *andreios*?

iii. If not, in what sense would Socrates have succeeded in identifying *andreia* with *epistēmē*?

iv. In the event, Socrates fails to convince Protagoras. He can no longer claim that *andreia* is *sophia* by claiming that a man always and only displays *andreia* in those actions in which he is exercising some *epistēmē*, or means-related knowledge. Robbed of this, how must Socrates now set about showing that *andreia* is *sophia*?

v. Would it be possible for a person incapable of forming sensible long-term goals (or at least of following such goals as imposed by others) to act with genuine *andreia*?

vi. Could this ability to form one's own or follow other people's long-term rational plans be reduced to a specialised *epistēmē*?

7. Protagoras does not attack the first part of the argument (see 3), but rather *G*. He points out, in effect, that Socrates has committed the logical fallacy known as 'illicit conversion': he accuses Socrates of arguing as if *A* – that all the *andreioi* are *tharraleoi* – entitles him 'illicitly' to assume the converse, *G*, that all the *tharraleoi* are *andreioi*, and so to conclude, *H*, that *sophia* is (the same as) *andreia*. Is Protagoras justified in saying that he had not said that the *tharraleoi* were courageous (see 5.iii–v)?

i. Protagoras said yes in answer to two questions:

(a) 'Do you call the courageous daring, *or something else?*'

(b) 'So what do you mean by the courageous? Did you not call them *the* daring?'

When he objects at 350c that he never agreed that the daring were courageous, to which of questions (a) or (b) was he referring?

ii. In XIV.6 we observed that when we say that mammals are air-breathers we are only committed to saying that air breathing is a characteristic which mammals have, but not a defining characteristic, since not all air breathers are mammals. (There are also reptiles, amphibians, etc.) But when we say that mammals are *the* creatures which are suckled at birth, the use of the definite article tends to introduce a defining characteristic such that not only are all mammals suckled at birth but *only* mammals are suckled at birth. We have seen that the plausibility of the present argument is dependent upon the insertion of 'the' into the statement 'the daring are [the] courageous' (see 5.iv–vi). Has Socrates unfairly worded his question so as to make it appear that (b) is only an innocent restatement of (a) (see 6.1) and so to lure Protagoras unwittingly to commit himself to a definition? Or is Protagoras trying to get out of trouble by exploiting the strict wording of the questions, ignoring the significance of his answer to (b), and concentrating on (a)?

iii. Would it in any case be fair for Socrates to point out that once Protagoras treats courage as a practical willingness to do dangerous things, he is vulnerable, so long as he accepts that *andreia* is *kalon*, to the kind of argument Socrates has presented?

8. Protagoras offers a *reductio ad absurdum* of Socrates' argument as follows:

Socrates	Protagoras
A: The courageous are daring.	*A₁:* The strong are physically powerful.
C: The knowledgeable are daring.	*C₁:* The knowledgeable are physically powerful.
G: The daring are courageous.	*G₁:* The physically powerful are strong.
H: Courage is wisdom.	*H₁:* Strength is wisdom.

Is this a fair analogy?

i. Is either argument even apparently valid?

ii. If H and H_1 are to be accepted as validly deduced, then two assumptions have to be made: (a) that the knowledgeable are daring/physically powerful, and (b) that the daring/physically powerful are knowledgeable. Of these Protagoras' version asserts only (a). Which steps in Socrates' original argument prove the second proposition (see 3)?

iii. Protagoras admitted that the daring without knowledge are not courageous. Could Protagoras have plausibly suggested that by analogy the physically powerful without knowledge are necessarily not strong?

9. Protagoras is maintaining that courage is a function partly of nature, partly of *proper training of the mind* (*eutrophia tēs psuchēs*). What does Protagoras mean by 'proper training of the mind'? (Reconsider 325b–d.)

i. At 313c Socrates described the sophist as a 'dealer in wares by which the *mind is fed*' (*psuchē trephetai*). In the light of that earlier conversation with Hippocrates, are Socrates and Protagoras likely to understand the same thing by *eutrophia tēs psuchēs*?

ii. Mental/spiritual training might consist of (a) the teaching of technical or intellectual excellence, (b) the kind of conditioning of attitudes which a child receives from parents or (c) the teaching of moral and spiritual excellence. Which of these definitions can Protagoras accept if he is still to maintain that excellence, including courage, is not connected with knowledge? On the other hand, which must he maintain if he wishes to argue both that excellence is teachable and that he is specially qualified to teach it?

10. Why has Plato made Socrates put forward an argument which is easily rebutted and never mentioned again? Is it because:

    (a)   The aim is dramatic: Protagoras, having had the worst of the previous arguments, needs to have his image refurbished?

    (b)   Socrates is using this argument to show that *andreia* must bear at least *some* relation to knowledge?

    (c)   Plato is illustrating for us the logical fallacy known as illicit conversion (see 7)?

    (d)   Socrates is trying to show what Protagoras would have to be committed to if he makes the extreme claim that *andreia* has nothing to do with the other *aretai*?

    (e)   This is the beginning of a process of elimination: having excluded the possibility that *andreia* is *sophia* in the sense that it involves simply having expert knowledge, Socrates is left with the second alternative to pursue (see 6)?

Section XXI (351b–353b)

1. What makes Socrates change the subject and move to the apparently unrelated question of *living well* (*eu zēn*)? (Reconsider XX.6; 10e).

2. Having agreed to Socrates' suggestion that a man who

lived his life to the end pleasantly would be said to have lived well, Protagoras then qualifies his assent by insisting that a man can be said to have lived a good life only if he takes his pleasure in *things worthy of respect* (*kala*). Why does he find this necessary?

i. Would you agree that it is good to live well?

ii. If all who have a pleasant life live well and all who have an unpleasant life live badly, then assuming that to live well is good and to live badly is bad, would it follow validly that living pleasantly is good (*agathon*) and living unpleasantly is bad (*kakon*)? If it does follow, what is wrong with concluding that living pleasantly is good?

iii. Suppose you were able to live in complete accordance with your wishes: would you say you were living well?

iv. If you answered no to (iii), do you mean that you would not wish to lead your life in accordance with your wishes? Or do you mean that we ought not to live solely in accordance with our wishes? How do these alternatives differ?

v. It is evident that some pleasures are considered less worthwhile than others: for instance, the pleasure of drinking is less *worthwhile* (*kalon*) than that to be had from being an accomplished pianist. Given this, would you agree with Protagoras that your answer to (iii) must depend on what your wishes are?

vi. 'A man who lives his life in accordance with his wishes lives well.' 'A man who devotes his life to worthwhile pursuits lives well.' Both these statements can seem true because the expression 'lives well' is in each case differently used. Explain the difference. Which kind of 'living well' corresponds with Socrates' original question, and which with Protagoras' qualified response?

Commentary

vii. We have stressed that *kalos* is a term of commendation at times interchangeable with *agathos*. But there are important differences. *Agathos* really means good in the sense of worthwhile or beneficial, and is contrasted with *kakos*, which means harmful or bad. *Kalos* leans more towards meaning admirable or attractive. Thus in theory it would be possible to think of some things as *agatha* without also thinking of them as *kala*. At 351c–d Socrates treats Protagoras' reservation as if it amounted to the proposition that some pleasures are bad, and Protagoras accepts this. If Socrates proves that all pleasure is good, will he thereby have succeeded in showing that all pleasure is *kalon*?

3. Socrates next rephrases his question by contrasting his proposition that something which is *pleasant* (*hēdu*) is, *qua* pleasant (that is, ignoring every other fact about it except the fact that it is pleasant), *good* (*agathon*), with the more generally held view that some pleasures are *bad* (*kaka*) just as some pains are good. Do you agree with the *polloi*, or do you think that *pleasure* (*hēdonē*), considered in itself, is good?

i. The word *hēdus* is generally translated as 'pleasant' and *hēdonē* as 'pleasure'. But *hēdonē* has wider connotations than just the gratification of material wants. A Greek would describe as *hēdu* anything which he would be glad to have. Thus not only sensory and sexual pleasure would be *hēdu*, but also political success, the good esteem of one's fellow citizens, victory at the Olympic games, even glorious death in battle. In English we might think of these things as admirable but we would probably not apply the word 'pleasant' to them. But a thing which is *hēdu* is something one would welcome or willingly choose – a choice-worthy or desirable thing. If *hēdonē* is considered in the wider sense of choice-worthiness

142

Section XXI

or desirability, is it plausible to say that a thing
which is *hēdu* to the extent that it is *hēdu*, is
agathon? Are the *polloi* and Protagoras understanding the word in the sense of choice-worthiness or in its narrower sense?

  ii. Is Socrates' argument based on a tautology? In
other words, is it true to say that, by definition, a
desirable thing is good? Or would it be possible to
have something which is choice-worthy but bad?

4. Is it the nature of a thing or activity which determines
whether it is (a) pleasant or unpleasant, and (b) good or
bad; or is it the consequences of the thing or activity?

  i. Drinking is *hēdu* but *kakon*; practising the piano
may be *agathon* but *aniaron* (unpleasant). Is it the
pleasure of drinking *qua* drinking which is *kakon*
or is it the consequences of drinking (hangovers,
liver disease, alcoholism)? (Conversely for practising the piano.)

  ii. Could it be said that the pleasure of drinking is
kakon, *qua* pleasure, on the grounds that it is
because of the pleasure of drinking that people
drink, and therefore sustain the consequent
illnesses?

5. Can Protagoras deny that it is *epistēmē* and *sophia*
which enable a man to choose between the best and
worst plans of action (see XX.6)?

6. Why does Socrates shift the focus of the conversation to
the subject of *epistēmē* and *sophia*?

  i. If *epistēmē* and *sophia* are the most powerful
human *aretai*, could we regard as *hēdu* something
which we knew to be *kakon*? Could we, in other
words, maintain that some *hēdonai* are bad?

  ii. If you know the best course open to you, could any
consideration make you choose an alternative,

143

and therefore less good, plan of action (see XIX.4)?

iii. If we assume that Socrates and Protagoras are thinking of *epistēmē/sophia* as the *aretē* which enables us to calculate the best plan of action, is it possible to say that a man can fail to perform the action which *epistēmē/sophia* recommends, being overcome by *hēdonē* (see 4)?

7. In this passage Socrates has sought to establish two points: that pleasure, *qua* pleasure, is good; and that whoever knows the best course of action will inevitably take it. In what previous themes in the dialogue do these propositions have their origin?

i. Re-read Socrates' speech about Simonides' poem and see XIX.4. How would you now answer XIX.4.iv?

ii. Socrates is trying to prove that *andreia* and *sophia* are the same. Reconsidering XX.6, do you think that a person who knows the best plan of action always acts courageously, if it is true that *epistēmē/sophia* is, as Protagoras put it, 'the most powerful of all human qualities'?

iii. Before the discussion was interrupted by the disagreement about the way the debate should be conducted, Socrates had been attempting to prove that it could never be *sōphron* to do what is *adikon*. His method was to try to show that this would involve saying that it would be *sōphron* for a man to take a worse plan of action when he might have taken a better. How might the supremacy of *epistēmē* and *sophia* affect his argument?

iv. Reconsider XVI.5; 9.ii–iii. Will the best plan always be *dikaion*?

v. The entire conversation between the two men arose out of a disagreement over whether *aretē* can be taught. Is (a) Protagoras' and (b) Socrates'

144

position here compatible with the points of view
they each adopted then?

vi. At 318e Protagoras claimed to teach good planning (*euboulia*), both of one's personal and of the
city's affairs. How would you now answer
VIII.3.ii?

8. How will Socrates refute the position of the *polloi*?

Section XXII (353c–358a)

1. See XXI.3.i. Socrates at 353d–e justifies his claim that
something *hēdu* must, *qua hēdu*, be a good by saying
that the only reason why something *hēdu* can be called
an evil is because it has consequences which are unpleasant. Would this, if true, show that Protagoras or
the *polloi* were mistaken in thinking that some things
that are *hēdea* are bad?

i. Suppose someone stays up all night at a party,
though he knows he has an important interview
in the morning. What explanation would the *polloi* give for this behaviour (according to Socrates)?
What explanation would Socrates (with the agreement of Protagoras) give?

ii. If there were something that was always regarded
as *hēdu* but that always had bad consequences,
hēdonē could not be called good (see XXI.3.i). Is
there such a thing?

iii. Reconsider XXI.3.ii. If we take the consequential-
ist view of value judgments and say that something is good or bad not in itself but depending on
whether it produces an overall balance of good or
bad consequences, and if, like Socrates, we say
further that a consequence is only and always
good if it is pleasurable (a doctrine known as He-

145

donism), have we reduced the proposition that all things that are *hēdea* are good to the status of a tautology? Has Socrates done this?

iv. If the *polloi* accept Socrates' explanation of why men call acts good or bad (354c–d), are they thereby obliged to give up their belief that 'some pleasant things are bad and some painful things are good' (351c)? Will they, for instance, have to give up the belief that drinking to excess is pleasant but bad?

v. Reconsider XXI.2.v–vii. Can things be good or bad for reasons other than that their consequences are pleasurable or painful for someone?

vi. Would a millionaire who devoted all his resources to the enjoyment of selfish and worthless (not-*kalai*) pleasures be said to have lived (a) pleasantly, (b) well? What would Protagoras say? What would Socrates say?

vii. Reconsider XXI.2.vii. If Protagoras accepts Socrates' claim that *hēdonē* is in itself a good, will he be obliged to give up his reservation that a pleasant life is a good only if it consists of pleasures which are *kala*?

viii. Suppose someone at Callias' house came away from this discussion and said to a friend: 'I've just heard the most shocking thing: Socrates thinks that a person can do anything he likes as long as he gets pleasure from it. That man would condone corruption, revolution and murder on the grounds that the person doing these things gets pleasure and benefit from them!' Would this man be justified in presenting Socrates' position in this way?

2. Here is a summary of the central argument of this section:

Assumption A: Some men adopt what they know to be a worse course of action led on by their desire for *hēdonē*.

Section XXII

Assumption B: The good (*to agathon*) is nothing other than *hēdonē* (or the absence of pain).

Assumption C: The bad (*to kakon*) is nothing other than pain (or absence of *hēdonē*).

Next Socrates substitutes *to agathon* for *hēdonē* (because of *B* and *C*). Note that he restates *A* in terms of wilfully choosing a bad action instead of failing to choose a better action, the two being taken as virtually the same in popular thinking.

Substitute *B* in *A*, giving

    D: Some men choose a *kakon* course of action, knowing it to be *kakon*, because they are led on by their desire for *to agathon*.

Substitute *C* in *A*, giving

    E: Some men choose a painful course of action, knowing it to be painful, because they are led on by their desire for *hēdonē*.

Assumption F: For any two possible courses of action, *x* and *y*, no man will choose *x* if he considers *x* more painful than *y*.

NOTE: Assumption *F* is an assumption of rational behaviour. It is a formal way of saying that, other things being equal, a man will always choose what he considers to be the most pleasant or least painful course of action open to him.

Conclusion G: *D* and *E* are absurd, and hence *A* is absurd.

Given the assumptions, is this a valid argument?

  i. Which of these assumptions, if any, is questionable?

3. Consider *F*. Is it true?

  i. Which would you prefer, which would be better: a week on the French Riviera or a week working on a car assembly line?

147

Commentary

ii. What considerations would convince you that it was better to spend a week on the assembly line? Do they amount to anything other than that you would be better off in the long run?

iii. Two men came upon a gold bar. 'I am rich already,' said one to the other, 'while you are poor. You take it.' Is this offer, in Socrates' terms, rational? Could the poor man rationally refuse?

iv. If a man chooses to lead a life of personal hardship because of his dedication to, say, writing poetry or alleviating sickness in a poor country, is he being irrational, or are there things other than personal pleasure such that to be deprived of them would involve mental anguish greater than the pain of physical hardship?

v. In the light of these questions, it appears that the answer to (3) must depend on just what we take to be pleasant and painful. When the *polloi* claim assumption *A*, in which sense do they understand *hēdonē*? What other senses might there be (see XXI.3.i)?

4. Consider *B* and *C*. Is the goodness of a thing the same as its propensity to produce pleasure?

i. The Socratic Paradox (XIX.4), in the hedonistic form in which Plato here presents it, may be used to argue convincingly that we always take what seems the best course open to us, to the extent that we are concerned only with our own interests. Can it be used equally convincingly to argue that a rational man will always act altruistically to the extent at least of not pursuing his own pleasure at the cost of harm to others?

ii. When the *polloi* claim *A*, Socrates seems to take them to mean that we can knowingly do what is bad *for us* because we are led astray by our desire for immediate *hēdonē*. Assuming that this is

148

what the *polloi* meant, in the light of (3) do you
agree with them?

iii. Suppose, on the contrary, the *polloi* meant:
> *Assumption A_1*: Some men choose a course of ac-
> tion which is bad *for someone
> else*, knowing it to be so, led on
> by their desire for *hēdonē for
> themselves.*

Will it now be possible to use B and C to generate
D and E (as in 2), in such a way that G still
follows?

iv. In Section XXI we saw how Socrates prepared the
ground for the acceptance of B and C. But now we
see that it is these assumptions which are the
most problematic for the validity of his argument.
What problems would we have to resolve in order
to know whether or not to accept B and C?

5. Let us modify F as follows:
> *Assumption F_1*: For any two possible courses of action,
> x and y, no man will choose x for his
> own ends if he considers x more painful
> than y for someone else.

This modifies your answer to 4.iii. A_1 now seems false.
Assumption F, we saw, was simply an assumption of
rational behaviour. Is F_1 also true of rational men?

i. Protagoras, in his explanation of the genesis of
politikē technē, said that we cannot survive on
our own without a *polis* and that the unrestricted
pursuit of self-interest makes political association
impossible. Could Protagoras therefore deny that
F_1 was rational?

ii. Protagoras professes to teach *politikē aretē*.
Given this distinction between mere self-interest
and enlightened (i.e. *polis*-serving) self-interest,
could Protagoras argue that Socrates has merely
shown that only in matters of immediate self-interest is it true to say that choosing a worse

149

Commentary

alternative is irrational and due to ignorance of consequences?

6. Of what things might a man have to be ignorant in order to be willing to take actions which were beneficial to himself in the short term but harmful to his *polis* in the long run?

    i. An Athenian businessman is honest in his personal dealings, shrewd and prudent, though willing to take sensible risks. He regularly makes the required sacrifices and offerings to the gods. Would a fifth-century fellow-citizen be willing to apply to him the terms *dikaios, andreios, hosios, sophos, sōphrōn*? Is he *agathos*?

    ii. It is his turn to be responsible for the equipping and manning of a warship to defend Athens. This is the Athenian equivalent of a wealth tax; he regularly evades it. Can he still be described in terms of these *aretai*? Is he an *agathos politēs*? (See VIII.4.i–ii; 6).

    iii. You might think that while he can no longer be called *dikaios*, he is, none the less, *sophos, sōphrōn, andreios* and (by conventional standards) *hosios*. Given Socrates' distinction between long-term and short-term *hēdonē*, why might even these epithets be withheld?

    iv. 'In my judgment it would be better for individuals themselves that the citizens (*politai*) should suffer and the *polis* flourish, than that the *politai* flourish and the *polis* suffer' (Thucydides. 2.60). Can a man exercise *sōphrosunē, dikaiosunē, hosiotēs, sophia* and *andreia* – in short, *aretē* – in matters relating to his personal interest, but not in matters of collective interest? (See VIII.3.iii).

    v. Reconsider 1.vii. Is Socrates' hedonism incompatible with socially (politically) responsible behaviour? Or might a man who held Socrates' hedonism be capable of regularly conforming to the legal and moral requirements of his *polis*, and of respecting the interests of his fellow citizens?

   vi. Will he inevitably and invariably behave in this way? Upon what considerations would this depend? (See 5.i).

7. Can ethics, or moral philosophy – the study of right and wrong – be described as a science of measurement?

   i. In the light of our discussion of 1.v, do pleasures differ only in intensity, or also in quality? Is there, in fact, any difference between Socrates' position and Protagoras' position at 351c, where the latter says that one's pleasure must be in things that are *kala*?

   ii. Socrates would have us believe that our choice of the best course of action is purely a matter of rationally calculating the consequences in terms of benefit and cost. Could a *polis* or individual expect to do well whose affairs are conducted on such a basis? Can decision-making be reduced, as Socrates claims, to an art of measurement (*metrē-tikē technē*) (356c–d)?

   iii. Granted that there might be a science whereby we could calculate the best course of action by measuring the likely pleasurable and painful consequences, could there also be such a science which would enable us to calculate what is *kalon* and *aischron*. Is it possible?

   iv. If ethics is a skill or branch of knowledge it ought to be possible to teach people what *to agathon* is and what *to kalon* is. Is it possible?

8. 'They all fell over themselves to agree that what had been said was correct.' Why?

   i. At 357e Socrates associates Prodicus and Hippias with Protagoras as being sophists, professed teachers of this science. Why does Plato have all three sophists make common cause, whereas they previously seemed to be jealous rivals?

ii. The idea that there is such an *epistēmē* has been arrived at by an argument about *hēdonē*: pleasure is of itself good because people make judgments about the goodness or badness of a thing exclusively in terms of its consequences, pleasant or painful. Therefore judgment of the choice-worthiness or otherwise of a thing is a matter of a sound knowledge of its consequences. We have seen, however, that without the extension of this reasoning (see 5 and 6) this argument might seem like rather shocking and crude hedonism (see 1.viii). Do Protagoras, Prodicus and Hippias fully understand the subtleties of Socrates' position? Are they willing to be seen as crude hedonists? Or has Socrates tricked them into appearing thus?

iii. If the trio of sophists look to the audience, now, like hedonistic opportunists, it must be admitted that Socrates is tarred with the same brush. And of course Socrates ultimately fell victim to the popular belief that he was a sophist. What in this passage looks like mere sophistry? Can we refute the charge that Socrates is merely using sophistic tricks?

Section XXIII (358a–360e)

1. Before launching into his final argument about *andreia*, Socrates recapitulates these points:

A: All actions which produce *hēdonē* are *kala*; hence *hēdonē* is *agathon* and *ōphelimon*.

B: No one who thinks he knows a better course of

action will choose a worse one (the Socratic Paradox).

C: Therefore, no one *hekōn* goes to meet what he considers *kakon*. (See XIX.4.)

Consider each in turn. Has Socrates in fact established all of them?

2. Reconsider XX.2.i–iv. Compare the following explanations of *andreia*:

   (a) The willingness to do what men fear.

   (b) The willingness to do what one fears oneself.

   (c) The willingness to do what men fear, in pursuit of an overridingly worthwhile end.

Which do you favour?

   i. If you favour (a), is it *andreion* for an experienced mountaineer to scale a rock simply because others who do not know how to climb are afraid to do so? If you reject (a), why do people nevertheless tend to think of such people as courageous? Must courage essentially involve overcoming fear?

   ii. If you favour (b): is the overcoming of fear always courageous, or does it depend on what the fear *is*? Is it possible for fears to be cowardly – or wise? If you reject (b), would it be courageous for a man with a fear of heights to overcome that fear?

   iii. If you favour (c), what quality will a man need in order to tell whether a given course is overridingly worthwhile? Is the *andreion* course of action always more worthwhile than any less *andreion* alternative?

3. Protagoras agreed that terror or fear are defined as the expectation of something *kakon*. Previously he had agreed that no man willingly goes to meet what he believes to be *kakon*. What, then, will determine whether a man is courageous or cowardly?

   i. If we accept both Socrates' definition of fear and

153

the Socratic Paradox, do we therefore have to reject the idea that the ability to conquer fear, or, in other words, to meet willingly what we fear to face, is an essential ingredient of courage?

ii. Why, then, according to Socrates, does a brave man face battle while a coward flees?

iii. What does the courageous man fear?

4. Has Protagoras' agreement that *andreia* is *kalon* (349e) made inevitable the conclusion that *andreia* is *epistēmē*?

i. Protagoras, who initially held explanation (a) for *andreia* (see 2), now finds that he would have to admit that in virtue of the Socratic Paradox and in violation of common sense, cowards and heroes alike flee the terrible (*to deinon*). He turns to explanation (b): A man fears war, he says, but 'courageous men are willing to go to war but cowards are not' (359e). Can he consistently maintain that a brave man fears war once he has gone on to agree that courageous men go to war because they consider it *kalon*? (359e)

ii. If fighting for one's country is *kalon* and if men who *know* what is *kalon* will choose it in preference to what is *kakon*, what is the difference between the courageous and the cowardly?

iii. See 3.i. Socrates' account of courage here appears to be not the conquest of fear, but the knowledge of what is *kalon* and *kakon*, in other words, knowing what is to be sought and what is to be shunned. From this point of view, is it courageous to fight for one's country? How would one decide?

5. See 1, point *A*. *Kala* acts (which courageous men seek to do) are *agatha* and *ōphelima*. Would it be fair to say that the courageous man is one who can properly judge the consequences of his actions and who chooses his actions accordingly?

Section XXIII

i. See XXI.7. Does the difference between the courageous man and the coward consist in the fact that (a) what one man considers desirable may be to another undesirable; or (b) one man may have a better knowledge of what is truly desirable than does the other?

ii. Is there any difference at all between a courageous man and man who is *sōphrōn*, *dikaios* – indeed, one who possesses *aretē*?

6. In Protagoras' creation story the excellences were explained as a necessary condition for human survival; they made cooperation possible. We also saw that Protagoras left it unclear whether he thinks of these excellences as non-rational, god-given instincts or conscious and rational principles. In the light of Socrates' arguments, which conclusion does Plato seem to favour?

i. If Socrates is right to argue that no man seeks evil willingly, what is the sole motive for human actions?

ii. Is that motive a non-rational instinct or a rational principle of conduct?

iii. A possible meaning of 'rational principle of conduct' is 'a justification for behaviour in terms of the pursuit of some desire or goal'. If so, it follows that the pursuit of *hēdonē*, since *hēdonē* appears to be an end in itself, and not to be pursued for the sake of something else, is a non-rational instinct. In what sense, then, would *andreia* be rational according to Socrates?

iv. Is it therefore rational to die for one's country?

v. *Andreia* is important because without it men could not combine in their war against the beasts, and would perish. If each individual is willing to risk death, then the *polis* is stronger and through its collective strength the individual's chances of survival are better. Do the excellences, then, simply amount to behaviour based on rational assessments of enlightened self-interest?

vi. Is *aretē* desirable because by exercising it men can pursue *hēdonē* (understood in the broad sense of individual and collective sense of well-being and security)? Or is *aretē* desirable in itself?

7. 'You seem utterly determined to get your way and have me giving the answers, Socrates.' Would Callias's guests conclude that Socrates has merely been interested in making Protagoras look foolish or has he arrived at a firm conclusion about the nature of *aretē*?

Section XXIV (360e–362a)

1. At 329c Protagoras, in answer to Socrates' question about the unity of excellence, had said 'Well, that's an easy question to answer, Socrates.' What does he now say? What has Plato taught us about the nature of moral discourse?

2. When Socrates argued that excellence did not appear to be teachable, he used the example of the Athenians who, he said, make a distinction between expertise or skill (*technē*: see VIII.4.i) on the one hand, and excellence (*aretē*: see IX.5.iii) on the other. However he now says that all of *aretē* is a kind of *epistēmē*. Assuming that he has proved this by his previous arguments, would you now say that *aretē* is a *technē*?

   i. If you say yes, would you say that there is really no difference at all between the nature of the body of knowledge a doctor needs and the body of knowledge a good man needs?

   ii. If you say no, nevertheless what important connection do you have to account for between a *technē* like medicine and a '*technē*' of excellence?

Section XXIV

3. Does Protagoras have any basis on which to claim that he can teach people to be good citizens both in their private and their public affairs (cf. 318e) even though he has tried to deny that all excellence is knowledge?

    i. Why was the argument that the excellences are closely related or identical crucial to Socrates' ultimate position that *aretē* is a particular kind of knowledge?

    ii. If excellence is a single body of knowledge, is it the kind of knowledge which Protagoras or the other sophists teach? What, by contrast with the courses of instruction offered by Protagoras, would a man teach who is, on Socrates' account of the matter, an expert in 'the proper training of the mind' (351b)? What, according to Plato, does Hippocrates need to learn in order to become 'a good man in truth' (339b) and a statesman?

    iii. If *aretē* is one body of knowledge and if 'knowledge' is to be taken in the sense of 'philosophical understanding', and if Protagoras continues to claim to teach *aretē* what would he have to be prepared to discuss if he agreed to continue the dialogue? Why is he reluctant to do so?

    iv. At 313e Socrates warned Hippocrates that it was only safe to purchase courses of instruction from someone with 'expert knowledge of the constitution of the mind'. Has Protagoras proved to have this kind of knowledge?

4. Socrates has previously praised Protagoras, and here Protagoras expresses his admiration for Socrates. In both instances is this praise sincere or ironic?

    i. Suppose the dialogue continued this way: '. . . And, as we were walking out I said to Hippocrates: "So now you see, Hippocrates, that Protagoras. . . " '. What are Socrates' conclusions about Protagoras?

Commentary

ii. If we could have overheard the conversation in Callias' house just after Socrates had left, what would Protagoras be saying to Prodicus and Hippias?

iii. If you conclude, in answer to (i) and (ii), that both men would be saying uncomplimentary things about each other, do you think that (a) in the light of the points each has made in the course of the debate and (b) considering Plato's characterisation of each man, both would be justified in their criticisms?

5. In his last long speech Socrates ends by saying that he is 'taking forethought for my entire life when I concern myself with all these questions'. Protagoras' last speech contains grudging praise for Socrates and a compliment to himself. Thus it is that the dialogue ends not with a conclusive statement about the issues which have been discussed but with a summary of the two men's view of themselves and their motives. What is the effect of this contrast?

6. Imagine a speech for Socrates, following on from the last line of his narrative, which began 'Therefore, my friend...'. Do you think that such a conclusion is needed to draw together the threads of the dialogue?

i. To Protagoras Socrates said that his only motive for continuing was 'to investigate the general subject of excellence and what excellence itself is'. What would he say by way of conclusion to his friend?

ii. In so far as the character of Socrates in the dialogue is Plato's creation, we can say that your answer to (i) would also answer, at least in part, a question about Plato's motives in writing the dialogue. But are there any motives which we can attribute to Plato which could not be expressed through Socrates' summary?

Section XXIV

iii. Suppose that instead of ending as it does the dialogue went on: '. . . As Hippocrates and I left Callias' house, Hippocrates said to me. . .'. What conclusions would Hippocrates have come to?

Biographical Index

Adeimantus, son of Cepis (315e): otherwise unknown.

Adeimantus, son of Leucolophides (315e): General under Alcibiades in 407 B.C. and again 406 and in 405, in Athens' crushing naval defeat at the battle of Aegospotami, after which he was taken prisoner by the Spartans.

Agathocles (316e): taught the celebrated Athenian musician and sophist Damon.

Agathon (315e): Athenian tragic poet born c. 450 B.C., died c. 400. Deeply influenced Euripides. Plato's *Symposium* takes place at his house.

Alcibiades (309a–c; 316a; 317d–e; 320a; 336b–e; 347b; 348b–c): Athenian demagogue, born c. 450 B.C., died 404. An aristocrat of the same leading family (Alcmaeonidae) as Pericles. The relationship between Alcibiades and Socrates has been much discussed. It seems that the adolescent Alcibiades had a crush on Socrates, who returned the affection in purely platonic terms (Plato, *Symposium* 218a ff.).

Andron, son of Androtion (315c): lifelong opponent of philosophy.

Antimoerus (315a): from Mende in Thrace. Otherwise unknown.

Antiphon: see Index.

Ariphron (320a): brother of Pericles.

Bias (343a): of Priene. Fl. mid-sixth century B.C.

Callias (311a; 314d–e; 315d; 317d; 335c–d; 336b–d; 338b; 348b–c; 362a): an Athenian aristocrat who inherited his father Hipponicus' large fortune in 424 B.C. and spent it

160

Biographical Index

lavishly on sophists and hangers-on. A notorious and fashionable dilettante.

Charmides (315a): an Athenian, son of Glaucon, cousin of Critias and Plato's maternal uncle. Portrayed in the *Charmides* as outstandingly handsome. In 404 B.C. he took part in the oligarchic government of Athens and died fighting against Thrasybulus' democrats.

Chilon (343a): a Spartan of the early sixth century B.C.

Cleinias (320a): an Athenian. The younger brother of Alcibiades and by reputation a complete madman.

Cleobulus (343a): of Lindus in Rhodes. Lived early sixth century B.C. His epitaph in honour of Gyges was scornfully condemned by Simonides (*Poeti Melici Graeci* fr. 581) as the work of an idiot.

Crison (335e–336a): of Himera. A runner who won at Olympia in 448, 444 and 440 B.C.

Critias (316a, 336e): an Athenian, son of Callaeschrus and reputedly a pupil of Socrates and close friend of Alcibiades. He was to become leader of the ruthless oligarchs who gained power in 404 B.C. Killed in 403.

Epimetheus (320d–322a; 361d); a mythological figure, son of Iapetus the Titan and Clymene; brother of Prometheus. His name means Afterthought.

Eryximachus (315e): an Athenian of the fifth century; son of Acumenus, a distinguished physician like his father, and a speaker in Plato's *Symposium*.

Eurybatus (327d): a proverbial rogue, apparently from Ephesus, who, on an embassy for Croesus of Lydia, went over to the enemy, Cyrus of Persia, with a large sum of money.

Herodicus (316e): from Selymbria in Thrace. Lived in the fifth century B.C. A sophist, specialising in both physical fitness and medicine.

Hesiod (316d; 340d): a poet of the mid-eighth century B.C. He wrote the didactic poem *Works and Days* (about farm-

161

ing) and *Theogony* (on mythology). He was held in much the same esteem as Homer.

Hippias (314c; 315c; 317c–d; 318e; 337c–338b; 342a; 347a–b; 357e; 358a; 359a; see Index): from Elis in the Peloponnese. A sophist of the mid-fifth century B.C. He had specialised in astronomy, but prided himself on being a polymath and rhetorician, and had a wide range of reputedly superficial knowledge and skill, and a talent for slick rhetoric laden with extravagant metaphor.

Hippocrates (310b–314c; 316a–c; 317e–319a; 328d): a young Athenian, Socrates' friend. Otherwise unknown.

Hippocrates (311b): of Cos. An Athenian of the fifth century B.C. The founder of a great school of medicine; hence the Hippocratic Oath.

Homer (309a; 311e; 316d; 340a): the earliest extant poet of Greece, about whose life virtually nothing is known. His two works, the *Iliad* and *Odyssey*, made him the equivalent of Shakespeare for the ancient Greeks. Many modern scholars believe these works were not written by a single author.

Iccus (316d): of Taras in southern Italy. Fl. c. 470 B.C. A famous athlete and gymnast.

Lenaea (327d): a winter festival held in the mouth of Gamelion (late January–early February) in honour of Dionysus. It included a competition of comic plays.

Musaeus (316d): a legendary and shadowy figure, believed to have been connected with the mystery cult of Eleusis in northern Attica.

Myson (343a): of Chen in Laconia (Sparta). Lived probably in the mid-sixth century B.C.

Orpheus (315b; 316d): the most important of the legendary forerunners of the Greek poets. He is supposed to have enchanted even the trees with the beauty of his music. His name is also connected with a chthonic mystery cult.

Orthagoras (318c): of Thebes in Boeotia. Little known outside this work.

Biographical Index

Paralus (315a; 328c): an Athenian. The younger of two illegitimate sons of Pericles. Shared with his brother the nickname 'boob-sucker' because of his feebleness.

Pausanias (315d): an Athenian, notorious homosexual pederast.

Pericles (319e–320a): Athenian politician, born early fifth century B.C., died in the plague of 428. A radical democrat who rose to be the greatest Athenian statesman of his time.

Phaedrus (315c): an Athenian. A friend of Plato, appears in the *Symposium*, and has a dialogue named after him. A devotee of oratory.

Pheidias (311c–e): an Athenian architect and sculptor who created the Parthenon at Athens and the temple of Zeus at Olympia.

Pherecrates (327d): an Athenian writer of comedy. His play the *Savages* was presented in 420 B.C. at the Lenaea. It does not however follow that the dramatic date of the dialogue is 419 B.C. Plato, writing in about 394 B.C., does not take into account precise chronological accuracy in setting a dialogue in earlier times, and often permits anachronisms.

Philippides (315a): an Athenian of a leading aristocratic family.

Phrynondas (327d): a person of proverbial badness.

Pittacus (339e–347a): of Mytilene on Lesbos, born *c.* 650 B.C., died *c.* 570. Statesman who rose to power in the political disorders of the late seventh century.

Polycleitus (311c; 328c): of Sicyon in the Peloponnese. A foremost sculptor of the late fifth century.

Prodicus (314c; 315c–316a; 317c–e; 336d; 337a–c; 339e–341e; 342a; 357e; 358a–e; 359a; see Index): of Ceos. A leading sophist of the fifth century. He specialised in the correct use of words, but also took an interest in science.

Prometheus (320d–322a; 361d): mythological figure, son of

163

Iapetus the Titan and Clymene, and brother of Epimetheus. His name means Forethought.

Protagoras: of Abdera in Thrace. Born *c.* 490 B.C., died *c.* 420. Most of our knowledge of him is derived from Plato's works, notably the *Protagoras* and the *Theaetetus.* He appears to have been the first sophist to claim to impart wisdom for a fee, and amassed large sums on his wide travels. He visited Athens on perhaps three occasions. On the first, he may have been expelled for his agnostic book on religion (see VII.2.iv). The second, presumably that referred to by Hippocrates at 310e, would have been around 544 B.C. when he was asked to write the constitution for a new Athenian colony founded at Thurii in Italy (see X.6.i). Assuming Protagoras' present visit not to be a fiction of Plato's, this would be the third. For details of his writings and teaching see VIII.5; X.6. i–iii; Index.

Pythocleides (316e): a well-known music teacher at Athens.

Scopas (339a): of Thessaly. A member of the powerful family of the Aleuadae, and patron of Simonides.

Simonides (316d; 339a–347a): of Iulis on Ceos. A lyric and elegaic poet.

Socrates: of Athens, born 469 B.C., died 339, son of Sophroniscus and Phaenarete. A shadowy figure who exerted a dominant influence on the intellectual youth of Athens in the last quarter of the fifth century. For knowledge of his life and teachings we rely mainly on a comic lampoon by Aristophanes and apologetic works of his admirers Plato and Xenophon. We can only say for certain that he was poor, and supported financially by his friends. He was brilliant at eristic debate, but turned the technique to the serious investigation of ethical questions. In addition he seems to have had a more mystical side, and to have been prone to deep trances. As a citizen he served with courage in the Peloponnesian war, and served as a council member in 406, when he courageously refused to countenance an unjust sentence of death against six generals, a sentence demanded by the democratic party. He showed similar courage in refusing to carry out an order of the Thirty Tyrants and arrest Leon of Salamis. He was finally sentenced to death by drinking hemlock in 399 B.C. For further details see VI.5; VII.2.iv; X.6.i; Index.

Solon (343a): an Athenian, *c.* 640–561 B.C. As *archon* in 594 he competely refomed the Athenian laws and was regarded as the constitutional founding father by both democrat and oligarch alike.

Tantalus (315c): mythical son of Zeus. He stole food from the gods and was aptly punished with everlasting hunger and thirst.

Thales (343a): of Miletus. Fl. *c.* 585. Earliest of the Ionian cosmologists, he was the first to predict a solar eclipse. He was also renowned as a statesman.

Zeuxippus (318b–c): of Heraclea, late fifth century B.C. He is probably none other than the painter Zeuxis, who, with Parrhasius and Polygnotus, was a foremost painter of his day.

Further Reading

The following is not intended to be a comprehensive bibliography, for which see Terence Irwin, *Plato's Moral Theory* (Oxford University Press, 1977).

Commentaries and Translations

J. and A. M. Adam, *Platonis Protagoras* (2nd edition), Cambridge, 1905 (Greek text with mainly linguistic and contextual notes)

W. K. C. Guthrie, *Plato's Protagoras and Meno*, Penguin Classics, 1956 (translation with fine introduction)

C. C. W. Taylor, *Plato's Protagoras*, Oxford University Press, 1976 (translation with detailed philosophical commentary)

G. Vlastos (ed.), *Plato, Protagoras*, Indianapolis and New York 1956 (Jowett's translation revised by Martin Ostwald; see Vlastos' Introduction)

Diels, H. and Kranz, W., *Fragmente der Vorsokratiker*, vol. 2, Berlin, 1952, reprinted 1960 (includes fragments of all the major sophists, including *Dissoi Logoi*, Antiphon's *On Truth* and Critias' *Sisyphus*)

Ferguson, J. and Chisholm, K. (eds), *Political and Social Life in the Great Age of Athens*, Wark Lock Educational, 1978, in conjuction with the Open University (includes translations of 'the Old Oligarch', Aristole's *Athenian Consitution* for the fifth century B.C., Antiphon's *On Truth* and Critias' *Sisyphus*)

Moore, J. M., *Aristotle and Xenophon on Democracy and Oligarchy*, Chatto and Windus, 1975 (translations with introductions and notes)

Further Reading

Other Works

Adkins, A. W. H., *Merit and Responsibility*, Clarendon Press, Oxford, 1960

Barrow, R., *Plato, Utilitarianism and Education*, Routledge, London 1975

Crombie, I. M., *An Examination of Plato's Doctrines*, Routledge, London, vol. 1, 1962, vol. 2, 1963

Crombie, I. M., *The Midwife's Apprentice*, Routledge, London, 1964

Dover, K. J., *Greek Popular Morality in the Time of Plato and Aristotle*, Blackwell, Oxford, 1974

Ehrenberg, V., *Solon to Socrates* (2nd edition), Methuen, London, 1973 (chs 6–8)

Gould, J. P. A., *The Development of Plato's Ethics*, Cambridge University Press, Cambridge, 1955

Guthrie, W. K. C., *A History of Greek Philosophy*, Cambridge University Press, Cambridge, vol. 3, 1969, vol. 4, 1975, vol. 5, 1978

Irwin, Terence, *Plato's Moral Theory*, Oxford University Press, Oxford, 1977

Robinson, R., *Plato's Earlier Dialectic* (2nd edition), Oxford, 1953 (chs 2, 3, and 5 reprinted in Vlastos (ed.), *The Philosophy of Socrates*

Taylor, A. E., *Plato, The Man and His Work* (4th edition), Methuen, London, 1937

Vlastos, G. (ed.), *The Philosophy of Socrates*, Doubleday, New York, 1971

Index

References in this index are exclusively to questions in the commentary.

Index

craft: see *techne*
daring: see *tharraleos*
de (but), XVIII.3
deinos (terrible), XXIII.4.i
democracy, IV.5–6; VI.4.ii
demos (people): see democracy
dikaios (just), *dikaiosune* (justice), X.6.ii; XI.5–7; XII.7.i;
 XXII.7.iii; XIV *passim*; XXI.7.iv; see also *ekklesia, adikia*
 (injustice), *adikos* (unjust), *adikein* (to commit injustice),
 XI.4.iii; XII.4; XIV.2; XIV.7; XVI.1–6; XVII.6.iii;
 XXI.7.iii; *dike* (justice) (derivatives: *dikazein, dikaste-*
 rion, dikastes), IX.5–7
Dissoi Logoi, VIII.5; IX.1.iii
ekklesia (assembly), IV.5–6; IX.4.ii
education, IV.4–7; V.1–3; VI.2; VII.2; VIII.3; VIII.6–7;
 IX.1.ii–iv; IX.4.iv; IX.6; XII.6; see also *eutrophia, math-*
 emata, sophists
eironeia (mock-modesty), XVII.3
elenchos (refutation), XIII.3; XIV.2. XIV.10; XV.1;
 XVIII.2.i; XVIII.5; see also logic and formal argument
emmenai (to be) (also *einai*), XVIII.3
episteme (knowledge), II.5.iii; XX.3; XX.6.i–iv; XXI *pas-*
 sim; XXIII *passim*; see also *sophia, techne*
ethics: absolute against relative standards of, X.6.iii–iv;
 XI.5.i–ii; XII.6.iii; XVI.7; XXII.7; XXIII.5.i; XXIII.6.vi; of
 education, see education, *polis*
eu (well), XVI.6.ii
euboulia (good planning, advice), VII.3; IX.3–4; IX.6.i;
 XVI.5; XXI.7.vi; see also *polis: politike techne*
euphronein (to exercise good sense), XVI.5; see also
 sophrosune
eu prattein (to do well), XVI.6.ii; XVI.6.iv
eutrophia tes psuches (proper training of the mind), XX.9;
 XXIV.3.ii; see also education
eu zen (to live well), XXI.1–2
excellence: see *arete*
fear, XXIII *passim*
genesthai (to become/to be), XVIII.3
good: see *agathos, kalos*
Hedonism, XXII.i.iii; XXII.4.i; XXII.6.v; XXII.7.ii–iii, see

169

Index

also *hedonē*

hēdonē (pleasure), *hēdus* (pleasant), XXI.2–7; XXII.1; XXIII.6.i–iii

hekōn (willingly), XVIII.3; XIX.4; XXIII *passim*

holy: see *hosiotēs*

hosiotēs (holiness), *hosios* (holy), XIV.1–2; XIV.7; *anhosios* (unholy), XIV.7; XX.2

justice: see *dikaios, dikaiosunē*

kakos (bad), I.4.i; XVIII.3; XIX.4; XXII.2; see also *aischros, agathos*

knowledge: see *aretē, epistēmē, sophia*

logic and formal argument (references are to both text and commentary), 311b–321a (III.2); 312c–e (IV.2–3); 319b–d (IX.2); 319d–320b (IX.4); 320d–323a (IX.6; IX.8); 320d–328d (IX.1–2); 323a–c (XII.3); 323c–324d (XII.4); 324d–326c (XII.6); 326e–328a (XII.7; XIII.1); 329e–330b (XIII.3–5; XIII.7); 330b–332a (XIV *passim*); 332a–333b (XV.3; XV.5–6); 333b–e (XVI.5–6); 333e–334c (XVI.7); 338e–348b (XVIII *passim*; XIX *passim*); 349a–350c (XX.1–6); 350c–351b (XX.7–8); 351b–c (XXI.2.ii); 353c–357c (XXII.2–5); 358a–360e (XXIII.1–3); sophistical argument, VII.3; XVII.7; XVIII.6–7; XIX.1.iii; XIX.4.iv; XXI.7.iii

mathēmata (courses of instruction), IV.7; V.i.ii; V.2; VIII.7; X.6.i; XXIV.3.iii, *amathia* (ignorance), *amathēs* (ignorant, untutored), XX.2–3; see also *epistēmē, sophia*

men (a Greek particle), XVIII.3

metrētikē technē (the art of measurement), XXII.7

moderation: see *sōphrosunē, aidōs*

nomos (law), XVII.6.iii; see also *dikaios: dikē*

ōphelimos (beneficial), XV.2; XXIII.1; XXIII.5; see also *agathos*

orthōs (correctly), XV.2

phusis (nature), XVII.6.iii

pleasure: see *hēdonē*

polemikē technē (warcraft); XI.4.i

polis (city), *poleis* (cities), VII.2.iv; VIII.4.i; XI.4.iv; XXII.5.i–ii; XXII.6; XXIII.6.v; *politēs* (citizen), VIII.7.iii; XXII.6.iv; see also *agathos politēs; politeuesthai* (to be a citizen); VIII.4.i; *politikē aretē* (political excellence),

170

Index

171